MARRIAGE BONDS

and

OTHER MARRIAGE RECORDS

of

AMHERST COUNTY, VIRGINIA

1763 - 1800

Compiled by
William Montgomery Sweeny

Notice

In many older books, foxing (or discoloration) occurs and, in some instances, print lightens with wear and age. Reprinted books, such as this, often duplicate these flaws, notwithstanding efforts to reduce or eliminate them. The pages of this reprint have been digitally enhanced and, where possible, the flaws eliminated in order to provide clarity of content and a pleasant reading experience.

Originally published:
Lynchburg, Virginia, 1937

Reprinted:
Janaway Publishing, Inc.
Santa Maria, California
2006, 2011

Janaway Publishing, Inc.
732 Kelsey Ct.
Santa Maria, California 93454
(805) 925-1038
www.janawaygenealogy.com

ISBN: 978-1-59641-010-7

Made in the United States of America

FOREWORD

Amherst County was formed from Albemarle County "and certain islands in the Fluvanna River," in 1761.

Albemarle County was formed from Goochland County and parts of Louisa "and certain islands in the Fluvanna River," in 1744.

Goochland County was formed from Henrico County, in 1728.*

Although Amherst County was formed in 1761, no marriage records have been found of an earlier date than 1763.

The abbreviation "M.R." used in the following pages means "Minister's Returns," i.e. returns of marriages celebrated by the different ministers and returned to Amherst Court according to law.

Anyone desiring to obtain certified copies of the marriage records in this book (except those taken from Pension Declarations), may do so by addressing the Clerk of the Circuit Court of Amherst County, Amherst, Virginia, and paying the required fee.

---

*See Robinson's: "Virginia Counties: Those Resulting from Virginia Legislation."

MARRIAGE BONDS and OTHER MARRIAGE RECORDS

of

AMHERST COUNTY, VIRGINIA

1763 - 1800

Abney, William, bachelor, and Milley Graves, spinster, December 19, 1785. John Taliaferro, surety. Consent of Gean Graves, mother of Milley.

Abny, John, bachelor, and Pattman Puckett, spinster, April 24, 1790. Jacob Puckett, surety. Consent of John Puckett, father of Pattman.

Adams, Charles, bachelor, and Mary Dawson, spinster, August 18, 1789. Benjamin Dawson, surety. Consent of John Dawson, father of Mary, for her to marry "Charles Adams, of Fluvanna County."

Adams, Richard, bachelor, of Fluvanna County, and Susannah Dawson, spinster, August 13, 1786. Benjamin Dawson, surety. Consent of John Dawson, father of Susannah.

Alexander, Joseph, and Sarah Reid, spinster, November 3, 1767. Alexander Miller, surety. Consent of Thomas Stuart.

Alexander, William, and Agness Reid, spinster, February 15, 1767. Alexander Miller and Andrew Reid, sureties. Consent of Agness.

Alford, John, bachelor, and Elizabeth Bibb, spinster, March 2, 1783. William Bibb, surety.

Alford, Thomas, and Frances Crisp, October 10, 1795. John Crisp, surety, who made oath that Frances Crisp (his sister) was 21 years of age. Certificate of marriage by the Rev. John Bonner, October 13, 1795. (M.R.)*

Allcock, John, bachelor, and Betsey Davenport, spinster, November 27, 1793. Richard Allcock, surety. Consent of Joseph Davenport, father of Betsey. Certificate of marriage by the Rev. William Dameron, December 6, 1793. (M.R.)

Allcock, Joseph Reynolds, bachelor, and Stilley Campbell, spinster, October 7, 1790. William Allcock, surety. Consent of Joel Campbell, father of Stilley.

---

*"M.R."—Minister's returns.

Allcock, William, and Caty Page, July 3, 1794. Gabriel Page, surety. Consent of Lucy Page, mother of Caty. Certificate of marriage by the Rev. William Dameron, July 3, 1794. (M.R.)

Allen, Daniel, bachelor, and Milley Huffman, spinster, February 20, 1787. Benjamin Powell, surety. Consent of Milley.

Allen, Hiram, and Elizabeth Paterson, May 13, 1800. Jabus Davis, surety. Certificate of marriage by the Rev. Wm. Crawford.

Anderson, David, and Elizabeth Hardy, married by the Rev. Benjamin Berger. Returned at a court held August 5, 1782. (Order Book 1782-1784, page 1.)

Anderson, Nelson, and Agness Crawford, March 18, 1799. John Horsley, surety. Consent of Nathan Crawford, father of Agness. Certificate of marriage by the Rev. William Crawford.

Anderson, Thomas, bachelor, and Betsy Hill, spinster, July 22, 1793. James Hill, surety. Consent of James Hill, father of Betsy.

Armistead, William, bachelor, and Sarah Meredith, September 21, 1795. Reuben Crawford, surety. Consent of Thomas Penn, guardian for William Armistead. Certificate of marriage by the Rev. Charles Crawford. (M.R.)

Arrington, John, and Susannah Bolling, August 8, 1796. Edward Bolling, surety.

Atkinson, Walker, and Rachel Sandidge, spinster, March 27, 1799. Waller Sandidge, surety. Consent of William Atkinson, father of Walker, who stated that his son was of age. Consent of John Sandidge, father of Rachel.

Atkinson, William, bachelor, and Betsey Gibson, spinster, August 13, 1787. Isaac Gibson, surety.

Austin, Joseph, and Jenny Alford, spinster, June 3, 1800. Benjamin Austin, surety. Consent of William Alford, father of Jenny. Certificate of marriage by the Rev. James Boyd, June 3, 1800. (M.R.)

Austin, Thomas, and Rebecca Turner, spinster, December 3, 1798. James Turner, Jr., surety. Consent of James Turner, father of Rebecca. Certificate of marriage by the Rev. William Crawford in the year 1799. (M.R.)

Ayres, Samuel, and Rachel Morrison, widow, November 9, 1772. Joseph Higginbotham and Benjamin Higginbotham, sureties.

Baber, Ambrose, bachelor, of Albemarle County, and Ailsey Bowman, spinster, March 5, 1787. Tilman Walton, surety.

Bacon, Ludwell, bachelor, and Nancy Long, spinster, December 21, 1794. Taliaferro Hill, surety. Consent of Lawrence Long. Certificate of marriage by the Rev. Ezekiel Campbell. (M.R.)

Bagby, John, and Matilda Davis, spinster, December 19, 1792. Isham Davis, surety. Consent of Matilda. Consent of Elizabeth Davis. The above parties were married by "the Rev. Mr. Crawford." (M.R.)

Bailey, Charles, and Jane Fitzpatrick, spinster, February 7, 1800. William Fitzpatrick, surety. Consent of her father, William Fitzpatrick, who calls her "Jana." Certificate of marriage by the Rev. Wm. Crawford. (M.R.)

Bailey, James, and Mary Wright, November 1, 1784. Richard Fulcher, surety. Consent of her mother, Mary Wright. Certificate of marriage by the Rev. Benjamin Coleman, November 10, 1784. (Order Book, 1784-1787, p. 59.)

Bailey, John, bachelor, and Mourning Wade, spinster, December 28, 1791. Jacob Petty John, surety. Consent of Mourning, who states she is of age. William Hughes also testifies she is of age.

Bailey, John, and Frances Turner, widow, December 28, 1772. Robert Page, surety. Consent of Frances. Consent of her father, John Lyon and of her mother (not named). Her father states that she is the widow of "Tere" Turner, deceased.

Bailey, John, Jr., and Polly Thurmond, spinster, August 15, 1797. John Turner, surety. Consent of her father, John Thurmond, John Turner made oath that he believed John Bailey, Jr., to be 21 years of age.

Bailey, Michael, bachelor, and Rose Wortham, spinster, September 22, 1796. William Wortham, surety.

Bailey, Samuel, and Ann Morrison spinster, April 21, 1800. John Farrar, surety.

Baldock, Reuben, bachelor, and Betsey Pendleton, spinster, September 9, 1793. Richard Pendleton, surety. Consent of her mother, Elizabeth Pendleton.

Ball, James, and Lucy Harding, spinster, March 6, 1797. William Bowman, surety, who made oath that James Ball and Lucy Harding were each 21 years of age.

Ball, William, widower, and Sarah Joplin, spinster, July 16, 1792. Ralph Thomas, surety, who testified that Sarah *Jopling* was over 21 years of age.

Ballenger, Henry, bachelor, and Polley Clarkson, spinster, August 4, 1788. John Clarkson, surety. Consent of his father, Richard Ballenger.

Ballinger, Achilles, bachelor, and Milley Hudson, spinster, May 5, 1787. Samuel Ballinger, surety. Consent of his father, Joseph Ballinger. Consent of her father, Joshua Hudson. Note: Her father, Joshua Hudson, in his will dated 1790, and probated 1801, calls her "Molly."

Ballinger, Joseph, widower, and Tabitha Ballow, spinster, April 3, 1782. Joseph Smith, surety. Consent of Tabitha. Certificate of marriage by the Rev. Benjamin Coleman, April 4, 1782. (Order book 1773-1782, p. 511.)

Ballow, John bachelor, and Mary Tunget, spinster, May 2, 1785. James Clemons, surety. Consent of Jery Tunget.

Banks, Reubin, bachelor, and Ann Hill, spinster, daughter of John
Hill, November 4, 1783. Charles Taliaferro, Jr., surety. Cer-
tificate of marriage by the Rev. Charles Clay, November 9, 1783.
(Order Book 1782-1784, p. 201.)

Banks, William, and Tamzin Landrum, October 24, 1775. Thomas
Landrum, surety.

Barnett, Alexander, bachelor, and Rachel Dawson, spinster, December
20, 1786. Samuel Lackey, surety. Consent of William Barnett.
Consent of her father, Henry Dawson.

Barnett, Rezon, and Elizabeth East, spinster, April 23, 1799. William
Jacob, surety. Consent of her father, James East. Certificate of
marriage by the Rev. William Crawford. (M.R.)

Barrett, Luke, bachelor, of Rockbridge County, and Jemima Buttery,
spinster, September 21, 1790. Robert Buttery, surety. Consent
of her mother, Sarah Buttery.

Battalsby, Noell, bachelor, and Elizabeth Hopper, spinster, March 20,
1786. Samuel S. Scruggs, surety. Consent of her father, Thomas
Hopper.

Bean, Leroy, bachelor, and Elizabeth Christian, spinster, November 7,
1792. Robert Holloway, surety. Consent of Elizabeth. The above
parties were married by the Rev. Mr. Dameron. (M.R.)

Bean, Richard, bachelor, and Nanny Phillips, spinster, daughter of
John Phillips, May 22, 1779, William Phillips, surety. Consent of
her father, John Phillips.

Beck, James, bachelor, and Amey Hughes, spinster, December 4, 1786.
John Campbell, surety. Consent of her father, William Hughes.

Beckley, John, and Susanna Ellis, widow, December 21, 1767. William
Horsley, surety. Consent of Susanna.

Becknall, Micajah, bachelor, and Pheby Landrum, spinster, October
23, 1782. Young Landrum, surety.

Bell, David, bachelor, and Mary Duke Christian, spinster, December
5, 1785. Charles Christian, surety.

Bell, Drury, bachelor, and Rachel Lee, spinster, January 9, 1789.
Gabriel Phillips, surety. Consent of her mother, Susanna Dameron. Consent of Joseph Dawson, John Wiatt and George Lee,
executors of William Lee, deceased.

Bell, John, and Susannah Littrel, May 21, 1792. John Fitzpatrick,
surety. Consent of her father, Richard *Littrell*. Certificate of
marriage by the Rev. Mr. Campbell. (M.R.)

Bell, Samuel, and Sally Mitchell, spinster, January 17, 1780. David
Shepherd, surety.

Bell, Samuel, bachelor, and Mary Barnett, spinster, October 10, 1781.
James Barnett, surety. Consent of her father, Robert Barnett.

Bennett, Artexerces, widower, and Mary Small, spinster, September
12, 1786. William Small, surety. Consent of Mary.

Bennett, John, and Rhoda Dinwiddie, August 10, 1798. James Hudley, surety. Consent of her mother, Eles *Hundley*. James Hundley made oath that John Bennett was 21 years of age.

Bethel, John, and Mary Elliott, spinster, December 4, 1797. Ezekiel Gilbert, surety. Charlotte Thompson made oath November 30, 1797, that Molly Elliott was 15 years of age when she came to live with her uncle, David Thompson,, deceased, husband of Charlotte Thompson, which was nine years ago; that she saw her age registered in a Bible at her mother's. Certificate of marriage by the Rev. Walter Christian. (M.R.)

Beverely, Francis, bachelor, and Mary Williams, spinster, November 29, 1792. Rolley Penn, surety. Consent of her mother, Nancy Williams.

Beverly, William, and Edy Pinn, November, 1800. The above parties were married by the Rev. James Boyd. (M.R.)

Bibb, Henry, and Nancy Parrock, June 21, 1783. Charles Parrock, surety. Consent of ——————— Parrock, either her father or mother (first name illegible).

Bibb, Martin, widower, and Nancy Cash, spinster, September 23, 1795. Reuben Crawford, surety. Martin Bibb made oath that Nancy Cash was over 21 years of age. Certificate of marriage by the Rev. Charles Crawford, 1795. (M.R.)

Bibb, Martin, widower, and Sarah Whitehead, spinster, December 5, 1792. Burcher Whitehead, surety. Consent of Sarah. Martin Bibb made oath that Sarah Whitehead was over 21 years of age. Certificate of marriage by the Rev. Mr. Dameron. (M.R.)

Bibb, Martin, bachelor, and Polly Gilbert, spinster, December 25, 1793. Gabriel Page, surety.

Bibb, Thomas, and Patsey Johnson, spinster, November 18, 1799. Randolph Cash, surety. Consent of her father, William Johnson. Randolph Cash made oath that Thomas Bibb was over 21 years of age. Certificate of marriage by the Rev. W. Crawford. (M.R.)

Bibe, Samuel, bachelor, and Ann Cartwright, spinster, November 2, 1789. Edward Ware, surety. Samuel Bibe stated that he was of lawful age. *Anny* Cartwright stated that she was of lawful age.

Bibey, James, bachelor, and Margery Baber, spinster, September 30, 1786. Richard Burnett, surety. Consent of Margery. David Witt states that Margery Baber is his wife's sister.

Bibey, Jolley, and Savery Harris, spinster, May 25, 1799. John George Weise, surety. Consent of her parents, John George and Elizabeth Weise.

Black, James, and Nancy Martin, spinster, April 3, 1797. Caleb Wiltshire, surety. Consent of his parents, Henry and Martha Black, of Rockbridge County. Consent of her mother, Elizabeth *Wilshire*.

Blain, George, bachelor, and Rachel Lyon, widow, July 3, 1769. Samuel Shackelford, surety. Consent of Rachel.

Blain, George, widower, and Eles Steven Rachel Masters, spinster, March 3, 1790. Samuel Hill, surety. Consent of Eles Steven Rachel.

Blaine, John, bachelor, of Albemarle County, and Jane Morrison, spinster, February 21, 1784. Thomas Morrison, surety. Consent of her parents, John and Jane Morrison.

Blair, Allen, bachelor, and Mary Ann Staples, spinster, December 14, 1778. John Staples, surety. Consent of Sarah Staples.

Blakemore, John, and Lucy Carter, widow and relict of Charles Carter, deceased, October 15, 1768. Job Carter, surety. Consent of Lucy.

Bolling, Bailey, bachelor, and Jean Carpenter, spinster, January 17, 1797. William Bolling, surety. Consent of her father, Benjamin Carpenter. William Bolling made oath that Bailey Bolling was 21 years of age.

Bolling, John, bachelor, and Elizabeth Moran, spinster, June 17, 1793. James Fulcher, surety. Consent of her father, Elijah Moran. The above parties were married by the Rev. Mr. Crawford. (M.R.)

Bolling, Robert, Jr., bachelor, and Susanna Watson, spinster, May 31, 1765. John Fraser, surety.

Bond, Nathan, and Ede Cash, married October 21, 1784, by the Rev. Joseph Ballinger. (Order Book 1784-1787, p. 60.)

Bond, Richard, and Susannah Mays, married May 15, 1783, by the Rev. Joseph Ballinger. (Order Book 1782-1784, p. 121.)

Bond, William, bachelor, and Margaret Davies, December 9, 1793. George Davis, surety. Consent of her father, David *Davis*.

Bonds, Jacob, and Jane Bedlecomb, June 10, 1795. Ruben Crawford, surety. Samuel Hill made oath that Jane Bedlecomb was 21 years of age.

Boush, Joseph, widower, and Mary Ann Bicknell, spinster, August 27, 1794. Consent of Mary Ann who signed as Mary Ann *Bicknel*.

Bowler, Austin, bachelor, and Lucy Church, spinster, September 13, 1796. William Smith, surety. Consent of her parents, Thomas and Sarah Church.

Bowling, James, Sr., and Lilly Moore Gillaspie, married April 7, 1777, in Amherst Co., Va. He was born at St. Mary's, Md., 1752; died March 12, 1836. His widow applied for a pension Sept. 4, 1838, aged 76 years. (From application in Veterans' Bureau, Washington, D. C.) There is no M.L.B. of record in Amherst.

Bowling, William, bachelor, and Sealey Mays, spinster, January 1, 1787. Sherod Bugg, surety. Consent of her father, William Mays.

Bowman, Marshall, bachelor, and Bethehland Jopling, May 19, 1794. Thomas Jopling, surety.

Bowman, Sherwood, and Elizabeth Harding, spinster, December 5, 1800. Alexander Horsebrough, surety. Consent of her father, Edward Harding.

Boyd, John, bachelor, and Frances Lyon, spinster, October 27, 1794. John Lyon, surety. Consent of her father, William Lyon. Francis Lyon made oath that John Boyd was over 21 years of age.

Brackenridge, John, bachelor, and Martha McAnally, spinster, July 12, 1791. Peter Flora, surety. Consent of her father, John McAnaly.

Bradley, Drury, bachelor, and Lucy Christian, spinster, December 6, 1784. James Stovall, surety. Consent of his father, William Bradley. Consent of her father, Robert Christian.

Bradshaw, John, bachelor, and Molley Loving, spinster, January 21, 1786. Bartlett Eads, surety. Consent of her father, John Loving.

Brannum, Edmond, bachelor, and Nancy Evans, spinster, December 6, 1790. Charles Christian, surety. Consent of Nancy.

Breaden, Thomas, bachelor, and Sukey Oglesby, spinster, June 18, 1788. John Oglesby, surety. Consent of Jacob Oglesby.

Bridge, John, bachelor, and Betsey Coffey, spinster, September 15, 1795. Edmond Coffey, surety. Consent of her father, William Coffey.

Bridgwater, Jonathan, bachelor, and Nancy Ewers, spinster, January 1, 1791. Thomas Ewers, surety.

Bridgwater, Nathaniel, and Patsey Clarke, spinster, August 20, 1798. Samuel Bridgwater, surety. Certificate of marriage by the Rev. William Crawford.

Bridgwater, Samuel, bachelor, and Hannah Wood, widow, April 24, 1789. Joseph Jopling, surety. Consent of Hannah.

Bridgwater, William, bachelor, and Sally Ewers, spinster, September 24, 1789. Thomas Ewers, surety.

Britt, William, bachelor, and Jemima C. Harden, June 16, 1794. Samuel Reid, surety. Consent of Jemima who signed as Jemima Haiden. James Reid made oath that Jemima Harden was 21 years of age.

Broaddus, Warner, bachelor, of Caroline County, and Polly Harris, spinster, December 13, 1790. James Pettitt, surety. Consent of her father, William Harris.

Brockman, Elijah, and Fanny Harrison, December 22, 1795. Reuben Harrison, surety.

Brown, Elliott, bachelor, and Catherine Ware, spinster, July 23, 1793. John Ware, surety. Consent of her mother, Mary Ann Lockhert. Certificate of marriage by the Rev. Mr. Crawford. (M.R.)

Brown, Henry, bachelor, and Mary Wright, spinster, October 20, 1788. Peter Carter, surety. Consent of her father, Isaac Wright.

Brown, James, and Milley Carter, spinster, September 25, 1800. Joseph C. Megginson, surety. Consent of her mother, Maryann Carter.

Brown, James, bachelor, and Winifred Brown, spinster, July 3, 1794. John Brown, surety. Consent of her father, John Brown. Certificate of marriage by the Rev. Ezekiel Campbell who calls the groom "James Brown, Jr."

Brown, James, bachelor, and Susannah Mills, spinster, May 30, 1795. John Lancaster, surety, who made oath that "Susannah Mills, daughter of Jesse Mills," had resided with him for some time and that he believed her to be 21 years of age.

Brown, James M., bachelor, and Rhody Powell, spinster, December 20, 1793. Samuel White, surety. Consent of her father, Wiatt Powell.

Brown, John, bachelor, and Mary Abney, spinster, July 18, 1789. James Brown, surety. Consent of Mary. John McAlexander and Alexander McAlexander testify that they have been acquainted with Mary Abney for several years past; that her father and mother are dead, and that they believe her to be 21 years of age.

Brown, Leroy, and Sally Grayham, spinster, November 23, 1800. Samuel Grams, surety. Consent of Thomas Grayham and John Brown, Sr. Certificate of marriage by the Rev. John Young, Nov. 26, 1800. (M.R.)

Brown, Moses, bachelor, and Milley Milstead, spinster, August 3, 1780. John Brown, surety. Joseph Milsted certifies that Moses Brown is a son of John Brown, of Amherst Co., and that Mr. and Mrs. *Milsted* consent to the marriage of their daughter, Milly, to Moses Brown.

Brown, Rice, and Nancy Hays, October 5, 1795. Thomas Lilly, surety. Rice Brown made oath that Nancy Hays was 21 years of age.

Brown, Samuel, bachelor, and Mary Laine, spinster, August 22, 1786. William Laine, surety. Consent of his mother, Rachel Brown.

Brown, Zachariah, and Susanna Rippetoe, spinster, July 25, 1798. William Rippetoe, surety. Consent of her parents, Peter and Sary Rippetoe. Certificate of marriage by the Rev. William Crawford. (M.R.)

Bryant, John, bachelor, and Elizabeth Staples, spinster, December 21, 1790. John Staples, surety.

Bryant, Martin, and Eliza Depriest. Certificate of marriage by the Rev. Will. Crawford. Not dated, but probably *circa* 1797-1799. (M.R.)

Bryant, Parmenas, bachelor, and Peggy Bibb, spinster, November 15, 1788. John Bibb, surety.

Bryant, Reuben, bachelor, and Elizabeth Mathews, spinster, January 10, 1795. Elijah Staton, surety, who made oath that Elizabeth Mathews was over 21 years of age.

Bryant, Richard, and Judith Staples, spinster, March 3, 1798. Parmenas Bryant, surety. Consent of Elizabeth Conner (mother) and Daniel Conner (step-father) of Richard Bryant, for him to marry "Judith Staples, daughter of John Staples." Consent of her mother, Agatha Staples. Certificate of marriage by the Rev. William Crawford. (M.R.)

Bryant, William, and Elizabeth Depriest, July 17, 1798. Wortham Eads, surety. Consent of her mother, Amy Depriest. William Eads made oath that Elizabeth Depriest was over 21 years of age.

Bryant, William O., and Pheebe Hambleton, July 6, 1797. James Hambleton, surety. Consent of her mother, Milly Hambleton.

Bryant, Zacharias, bachelor, and Tabatha Stinett, spinster, March 7, 1787. Charles Wilsher, surety. Consent of her father, John Stinett.

Brydie, Alexander, bachelor, and Nancy C. Penn, spinster, December 17, 1795. W. S. Crawford, surety.

Bucknall, John, bachelor, and Ann Stoneham, spinster, September 16, 1788. Micajah Bucknall, surety. Consent of her father, George Stoneham.

Burford, Ambrose, bachelor, and Nancy Tinsley, spinster, January 19, 1796. Archibald Burford, surety. Consent of her father, David Tinsley.

Burford, James, bachelor, and Mary Rucker, spinster. Certificate of marriage October 1, 1782, by the Rev. Charles Clay. (Order Book 1782-1784, page 107.)

Burford, Philip, bachelor, and Peggy Rucker, widow, April 12, 1791. Ambrose Burford, surety. Consent of Peggy.

Burk, Joseph, bachelor, and Maryann Campbell, spinster, October 28, 1789. Laurence Campbell, surety.

Burks, David, Jr., and Betsey Phillips Thomas, spinster, October 1, 1799. Mathew Roberts, surety. Consent of John Thomas. Samuel Burks (son of David Burks) made oath that David Burks was 21 years of age.

Burks, Lindsey, and Polly Burks, December 9, 1797. David Burks, surety. Consent of her father, Charles Burks. Certificate of marriage by the Rev. Charles Crawford. (M.R.)

Burks, Richard, bachelor, and Polly Harris, spinster, June 9, 1795. John Harris, surety. Certificate of marriage by the Rev. William Crawford. (M.R.)

Burks, Richard, and Elizabeth Roach, December 30, 1797. Ransom Gatewood, surety. Consent of her father, Ashcraft Roach.

Burks, Samuel, bachelor, and Peggy Parks, spinster, December 21, 1789. William Tinsley, surety. Consent of her mother, Mary Parks. Consent of Zach. Dawson, guardian.

Burks, William, bachelor, and Nancy Roberts, spinster, September 15, 1794. Henry Roberts, surety, who requests the Clerk to issue a marriage license for William Burks to marry Nancy Roberts, daughter of Elliott Roberts, deceased.

Burnett, John, and Patsey Ballow, spinster, October 17, 1799. William Burnett, surety, who made oath that John Burnett was 21 years of age.

Burnett, Micajah, bachelor, and Sally McDaniel, spinster, January 29, 1789. Jesse Fortune, surety. Consent of Pashe Mack Alexander, mother of "Sally Mack Dannel." Consent of Bond Burnett, father or mother of Micajah.

Burnett, Richmond, bachelor, and Nancy Harris, spinster, July 31, 1793. John Harris, surety. Consent of her father, John Harris. Certificate of marriage by the Rev. Mr. Dawson, who calls the groom, "Richard Burnett." (M.R.)

Burnett, William, and Elizabeth Berlow, spinster, September 2, 1797. John Layne, surety. John Layne (waterman), made oath that William Burnett and Betsey Berlow were each 21 years of age.

Burrus, Joseph, bachelor, and Sophia Rucker, seamstress, January 9, 1792. Will Loving, Jr., surety. Consent of her father, Benjamin Rucker.

Burton, Philip, bachelor, and Ann Jones, spinster, married October 30, 1783, by the Rev. Charles Clay. (Order Book 1782-1784, p. 201).

Burton, William, bachelor, and Frances Penn, spinster, March 6, 1780. Edmund Wilcox, surety.

Bush, John, of Fluvanna County, widower, and Mary Tilman, spinster, May 7, 1782. William Walton, surety. Consent of Thomas Tilman, of Fluvanna County. Certificate of marriage by the Rev. Benjamin Coleman, May 9, 1782. (Order Book 1773-1782, page 512.)

Buster, Claudius, and Nancy Moffitt, March 19, 1798. John Merritt, surety. Consent of her guardian, Philip Johnson.

Buster, William, bachelor, and Mary Moffett, spinster, May 21, 1792. William Turner, surety. Consent of her guardian, Philip Johnson. Certificate of marriage by the Rev. Mr. Crawford. (M.R.)

Cabell, George, Jr., and Susanna Wiatt, January 13, 1798. Thomas W. Cocke, surety. Consent of her father, John Wiatt, for her to marry "Dr. George Cabell, Jr."

Cabell, Landon, bachelor, and Judith S. Rose, spinster, November 7, 1794. Samuel Irvine, surety.

Cabell, William, Jr., and Elizabeth Cabell, spinster, April 6, 1795. Landon Cabell, surety. Consent of her father, W. Cabell.

Caffey, William, bachelor, and Sally Turner, spinster, August 10, 1796. Joseph Newman, surety, who made oath that Sally Turner, daughter of John Turner, was 21 years of age.

Caffrey, John, and Mary Donalson, October 25, 1775. Samuel Hairston, surety. Consent of her father, John *Donelson.*

Callaway, James, Jun., of the County of Campbell, and Betsy Shepherd (relict of David Shepherd, deceased), January 13, 1784. Gabriel Penn, surety. Consent of Betsy. Bourne Price testified that he believed James Callaway to be over 21 years of age. Gabriel Penn testified that James Callaway was over 21 years of age.

Calvert, Christopher, bachelor, and Elizabeth Cox, spinster, January 3, 1791. David Tinsley, surety. Consent of her father, Volintine Cox.

Camden, John, bachelor, and Franky Phillips, spinster, March 19, 1796. John Phillips, surety.

Camden, Micajah, bachelor, and Mary Garland, spinster, January 23, 1793. Owen Haskins, surety. Consent of her mother, Ann Harper. Certificate of marriage by Rev. Mr. Crawford. (M.R.)

Camden, William, Jr., and Polly Ware, spinster, April 1, 1800. James Wood, surety. Consent of her father, John Ware.

Cameron, Allen, bachelor, and Jane Dempsey, spinster, December 21, 1795. Duncan Cameron, surety. Thomas Spencer made oath that Jane Dempsey was 21 years of age. Certificate of marriage by the Rev. William Crawford. (M.R.)

Camp, Abraham, and Betsy Humbles, August 15, 1793. John Redcross, surety. Consent of Amy Humbles.

Camp, Samuel, and Mary Banks, spinster, November 12, 1776. David Shepherd, surety. Consent of her father, Gerrard Banks.

Campbell, Ambrose, and Nancy Gillaspie, spinster, July 2, 1799. George Gillaspie, surety.

Campbell, Anthony, and Ann Ware. Certificate of marriage by the Rev. Benjamin Berger, in the year 1782. Returned at a court held August 5, 1782. (Order Book 1782-1784, p. 1.)

Campbell, Daniel, bachelor, and Sarah Forbus, spinster, April 9, 1784. Robert Mays, surety. Consent of Sarah.

Campbell, Ezekiel, bachelor, and Jane Moran, spinster, November 10, 1791. Littleberry Witt, surety. Consent of her father, Nicholas Moran.

Campbell, George, bachelor, and Anne Depriest, spinster, September 20, 1791. John Depriest, surety. Consent of her mother, Anne Depriest. Consent of Anne.

Campbell, George, Jr., bachelor, and Eady Whitehead, spinster, November 19, 1794. George Campbell, Sr., surety. Consent of his father, George Campbell, Sr. Certificate of marriage by the Rev. Ezekiel Campbell. (M.R.)

Campbell, Hugh, widower, and Elizabeth Barrett, widow, November 9, 1795. William Barrett, surety. Consent of Elizabeth. Certificate of marriage by the Rev. Charles Crawford. (M.R.)

Campbell, James, and Sarah Moran, spinster, March 17, 1800. Nicholas Moran, surety. Certificate of marriage by the Rev. William Crawford. (M.R.)

Campbell, James, and Christian Patterson, married by the Rev. Mr. Campbell, 1793. (M.R.) No M.L.B.

Campbell, Joel, and Peggy Patterson, June 13, 1799. Samuel Campbell, surety. Consent of his mother, Caty Campbell. Consent of her mother, Betsey Patterson. Certificate of marriage by the Rev. William Crawford. (M.R.)

Campbell, John, and Milley Coffee, February 22, 1793. Thomas Bradey, surety. Consent of Frances Campbell as to John and stated he was of age. William Coffey stated that Milley was 21 years of age.

Campbell, Joseph, and Sarah Moran. Certificate of marriage by the Rev. W. Crawford in the year 1798. (M.R.)

Campbell, Patrick, of Botetourt County, and Ann Powell, spinster, November 3, 1774. James Ware, surety.

Campbell, Samuel, bachelor, and Christian Patterson, spinster, January 21, 1793. Benjamin Camden, surety. Consent of her mother, Betsy Patterson.

Campbell, Wiley, and Elizabeth N. Sale, spinster, November 18, 1800. John Sale, surety. Certificate of marriage by the Rev. James Boyd. (M.R.)

Canady, Moses, bachelor, and Nancy Garner, spinster, October 27, 1789. Charles Taliaferro, surety. Consent of Nancy.

Carey, Daniel, and Susannah Fox, spinster, November 1, 1799. William Carey, surety. Consent of her parents, Samuel and Elizabeth Fox.

Carey, William, and Betsey Choop, widow, November 1, 1799. Daniel Carey, surety, who made oath that William Carey and Betsey Choop were both of age.

Carpenter, Enoch, bachelor, and Sally Evans, spinster, October 20, 1794. Wm. Evans, surety.

Carpenter, George, and Jane Phillips, spinster, November 3, 1797. John Phillips, surety. John Davis made oath that George Carpenter was over 21 years of age. Certificate of marriage by the Rev. Charles Crawford. (M.R.)

Carpenter, Hensley, and Rhody Mays, spinster, November 3, 1797. Benjamin Carpenter and Robert Mays, sureties. Certificate of marriage by the Rev. Charles Crawford. (M.R.)

Carpenter, James, and Susanna Hill, February 14, 1798. James Fulcher, surety. Consent of her mother, Elizabeth Hill, widow.

Carr, John, and Christian Phillips. Certificate of marriage by the Rev. Benjamin Berger, 1782. Returned at a court held August 5, 1782. (Order Book 1782-1784, p. 1.)

Carter, Abraham, bachelor, and Mary Roberts, spinster, February 15, 1787. John Taliaferro, surety. Consent of her father, "Josh" Roberts.

Carter, Charles, bachelor, and Lucy Goodwin, spinster, November 26, 1788. Benjamin White, surety. Consent of her mother, Mary Goodwin.

Carter, Edward, and Nancy Wright, spinster, May 7, 1799. James Browne, surety. Consent of her father, Isaac Wright.

Carter, Edward, bachelor, and Ann Vaughan, widow, September —, 1782. Peter Carter, surety. Consent of Ann. Certificate of marriage by the Rev. Benjamin Coleman, September 23, 1782. (Order Book 1782-1784, p. 65.)

Carter, Jesse, bachelor, and Frances Lucas, spinster, May 28, 1793. Ambrose Rucker, surety. Consent of Frances. Certificate of marriage by the Rev. Mr. Crawford. (M.R.)

Carter, John, bachelor, and Sally Day, spinster, April 6, 1791. John Day, surety. Consent of his mother, Mary Carter, who stated that he was over 21 years of age. Consent of her mother, Maryann Day. Consent of her brother, Samuel Day.

Carter, Landon, and Mary Goodrich were married by the Rev. Benjamin Coleman, March 22, 1782. (Order Book 1773-1782, p. 511.)

Carter, Peter, bachelor, and Delphy Sandidge, spinster, September 11, 1793. Waller Sandidge, surety. Consent of John Sandidge. Certificate of marriage by the Rev. Mr. Crawford. (M.R.)

Carter, Peter, bachelor, and Elizabeth Sandidge, spinster, September 3, 1787. Abraham Carter, surety.

Carter, William, and Caty Williams were married by the Rev. Benjamin Coleman, April 4, 1782. (Order Book 1782-1784, p. 511.)

Carter, William, and Bettie Elliss were married by the Rev. Benjamin Coleman, June 4, 1784. (Order Book 1782-1784, p. 306.)

Cartwright, John, widower, and Martha Patterson, spinster, July 31, 1779. George Galaspie, surety. Consent of Martha.

Cartwright, Peter, bachelor, and Christian Garvin, spinster, February 27, 1787. William Cartwright, surety. Consent of Christian.

Cash, Howard, bachelor, and Sally Gillespie, spinster, January 16, 1792. George Gillespie, surety.

Cash, James, and Nancy Wright, October 20, 1792. Joel Swinney, surety. Consent of her father, Moses Wright. "James Cash and *Mary* Wright married by the Rev. Mr. Crawford." (M.R.)

Cash, Joel, bachelor, and Elizabeth Rogers, spinster, November 2, 1795. Thomas Powell, surety. Consent of her father, Benjamin Rogers. Certificate of marriage by the Rev. Charles Crawford. (M.R.)

Cash, John, bachelor, and Sally Wortham, spinster, November 10, 1795. George Dillard, surety. Consent of her father, George Wortham. Certificate of marriage by the Rev. Charles Crawford. (M.R.)

Cash, John, and Lucy Campbell, January 23, 1782. He was born in Amherst, April 5, 1757; died August 13, 1836. She was born March 3, 1760. (From pension application.)

Cash, Peter, bachelor, and Ann Holliday, spinster, June 16, 1789. John Holladay, surety.

"S^r this is to let you no that all Partes is a greeable that Peter Cash and Ann Holladay should be married
Mr Wm Loving   Peter Cash   seal.
Test. John Holloday   Fielden Holloday."

Cash, Randolph, bachelor, and Sally Bibb, spinster, January 1, 1794. Alexander Marr, surety. Consent of her mother, Elizabeth Bibb.

Cash, William, bachelor, and Jane Patterson, spinster, June 4, 1781. Linn Banks, surety. Stephen Cash certifies that his son, William, is 21 years of age.

Cash, William, and Sally Campbell, spinster, November 7, 1797. Joel Campbell, surety. Consent of her mother, Caty Campbell, widow.

Cashwell, Henry, bachelor, and Catey Grady, spinster, December 4, 1786. John Campbell (hatter), surety. Consent of Philip and Mildred Goyn. Consent of Catey.

Cashwell, William, bachelor, and Betsey Penn, spinster, November 7, 1791. Moses Penn, surety.

Caszeal, William, and Ann Waters, married February 2, 1783, by the Rev. Benjamin Coleman. (Order Book 1782-1784, p. 102.)

Chamberlain, William, and Mary Ann Nevil, widow, September 4, 1780. Sherred Moore Galaspie, surety. Consent of Mary Ann.

Chappell, John, and Sally Shelton, spinster, December 29, 1800. Lewis Dawson, surety. Consent of her father, Richard Shelton.

Chastaine, James, and Phoebee Pagett were married by the Rev. Benjamin Coleman, April 18, 1782. (Order Book 1773-1782, p. 511.)

Cheatham, John, and Sarah Thurmond, spinster, February 2, 1799. Leonard Cheatham, surety. Consent of her father, Guttridge Thurmond.

Chewning, John, and Polly Pugh, spinster, February 18, 1799. James Pugh, surety. Consent of her father, John Pugh.

Childres, John, bachelor, and Sally Goode, spinster, December 19, 1794. William Henderson, surety. Consent of her father, Benjamin Goode.

Childress, Benjamin, bachelor, and Maryann McCabe, spinster, January 19, 1791. William Staton, surety. Consent of her mother, Sarah McCabe. Consent of Maryann.

Childress, Goolsbey, and Nancy Swinney, were married by the Rev. Benjamin Coleman, February 28, 1782. (Order Book 1773-1782, p. 511.)

Childress, Jesse, bachelor, and Annes Sandidge, October 13, 1792. Robert Tucker, surety. Consent of her father, John Sandidge. Certificate of marriage by the Rev. Mr. Crawford. (M.R.)

Childress, Major, and Hannah Ballew, January 19, 1796. Joseph Higginbotham, surety. Consent of his father, Joseph Childress, Sr., who states that his son is under age. Consent of her father, Stewart Ballew.

Childress, Reubin, bachelor, and Margaret Hudson, spinster, October 7, 1785. Elisha Dennis, surety. Consent of his father, Joseph Childress.

Childress, Robert, and Nancy Pryor, were married by the Rev. Benjamin Coleman, March 27, 1783. (Order Book 1782-1784, p. 111.)

Childress, Thomas, bachelor, and Elizabeth Atkinson, spinster, January 8, 1796. Alexander McAlexander, surety. Consent of her guardian, James Alexander, who stated she was of age. Certificate of marriage by the Rev. William Crawford. (M.R.)

Christian, Charles H., and Jenny Huckstep, June 12, 1796. Consent of Will Cabell, Jr. Samuel Huckstep, surety.

Christian, Drury, bachelor, and Mornin Christian, spinster, March 14, 1785. James Gresham, surety. Consent of his father, Robert Christian. Consent of Mornin .

Christian, George, and Martha Bell, spinster, January 16, 1775. Henry Bell, surety.

Christian, H., and Gilly Owen. Certificate of marriage by the Rev. W. Christian, 1799. (M.R.)

Christian, Henry, and Polly Owens, spinster, March 5, 1800. Barnett Owens, surety.

Christian, James, bachelor, and Cordelia Watts, spinster, February 28, 1795. John London, surety. Consent of Reuben Norvell and Stephen Watts, guardians.

Christian, James, bachelor, and Mary Christian, December 6, 1790. Drury Christian, surety. Consent of her mother, Mary Christian. Consent of Mary.

Christian, Turner, widower, and Elizabeth Leek, widow, October 6, 1788. John Christian, surety. Consent of her father, Philip Penn.

Clark, Andrew, bachelor, and Sarah Hansbrough, spinster, June 11, 1781. John Ball, surety. Consent of her mother, Keziah Hansbrough.

Clark, James, and Sarah Fitzpatrick, January 21, 1799. William Fitzpatrick, surety.

Clark, Joseph, and S. F. Patrick. Certificate of marriage by the Rev. William Crawford, 1799. (M.R.)

Clark, Leonard, and Sally Williams, March 12, 1796. William Clarke, surety.

Clark, Nathaniel, and Mary Lemaster, spinster, March 13, 1792. William Brill, surety, who made oath that Mary Lemaster was over 21 years of age.

Clark, William, bachelor, and Nancy Williams, spinster, September 3, 1794. Leonard Clark, surety.

Clarke, George, bachelor, and Levisay Evins, May 13, 1795. Leonard Clarke, surety. Consent of her mother, Hannah *Ivins.*

Clarke, Joseph, and Susannah Middlebrook, September 25, 1792. Consent of Susannah who stated that she was of lawful age.

Clarkson, James, bachelor, and Elizabeth Jacobs, spinster. November 7, 1785. John Jacobs, surety.

Clarkson, Nelson, bachelor, and Milley Loving, spinster, August 21, 1792. John Loving, Jr., surety. Consent of her mother. Betty

Loving. Consent of Will Loving and John Loving, Jr., brothers of Milley.

Clarkson, William, bachelor, and Elizabeth Mantiply, October 27, 1795. Nathaniel Mantiply, surety. Consent of his father, John Clarkson. Certificate of marriage by the Rev. Charles Crawford. (M.R.)

Clarkson, William, and Lucinda Franklin, February 17, 1798. Jeremiah Franklin, surety.

Clasbey, Thomas, and Catherine Bourn, spinster, December 22, 1800. William Clasbey, surety. Consent of her father, Henry Bourn. Certificate of marriage by the Rev. James Boyd. (M.R.)

Clements, Jesse, bachelor, and Elizabeth Coleman, spinster, February 5, 1787. James Coleman, surety. Consent of William Coleman and William Clement for Jesse *Clement* to marry Elizabeth Coleman, daughter of Millian Coleman.

Clements, John, bachelor, and Jane Mills Key, spinster, August 20, 1787. William Key, surety. Consent of her father, Martin Key. Consent of his father, William Clements.

Clements, John, bachelor, and Mary Midlock Dodd, spinster. October 28, 1791. Joseph Dodd, surety.

Clements, Thomas, and Rosanna Tinsley, spinster, March 10, 1800. Francis Clements, surety. Consent of her father, Joshua Tinsley. Samuel Clements made oath that Thomas Clements was 21 years of age.

Coatney, Samuel, and ———— Baddow. Certificate of marriage by the Rev. Leonard Ballow, Sept., 1797. (M.R.) See *Samuel Courtney.*

Cocke, Thomas W., of Campbell County, and Sally Crawford, spinster, January 15, 1799. George Cabell, Jr., surety. Consent of her father David Crawford.

Coffee, William, and Betsey Giles, April 18, 1800. Edmond Coffee, surety, who made oath that William Coffee was over 21 years of age. Certificate of marriage by the Rev. Wm. Crawford. (M.R.)

Coffey, Edmund, and Tildy Fitzgerald, spinster, January 3, 1798. Edmund Coffey, surety. Consent of her mother, Caty Duncan and her step-father, James Duncan. Edmund Coffey, Jr., made oath that Edmund Coffey, son of Edmund Coffey, was 21 years of age.

Coffey, Osborn, bachelor, and Mary Nightingale, spinster, February 15, 1783. John Jones, surety. Consent of her father, Matthew Nightingale.

Coffey, William, Jr., bachelor, and Polly Rippeto, spinster, November 2, 1790. James Rippeto, surety. Consent of Peter Rippeto.

Coleman, Daniel, and Mary Wilson, spinster, November 26, 1798. Jonathan Wilson, surety.

Coleman, James, bachelor, and Anne Childress, spinster, July 15, 1786. Thomas Coleman, surety. Consent of Anne who states she is of lawful age.

"Sir Please to deliver marriage Lisense to James Coleman and Nancy Childress & you much oblige your Humble Servt
Milley Coleman.
Test. Thomas Coleman, Thomas Lucas."

Coleman, Jesse, bachelor, and Susannah Peter, November 4, 1789. Thomas Garland, surety.

"Sir
Be pleased to let Jesse Coleman son of William Coleman and Susannah Peter daughter of William Peter have license of matrimony, &c.
William Peter.
William Coleman.
Nov. 4, 1789.
Test. James Coleman."

Coleman, Joseph, bachelor, of Spotsylvania County, and Elizabeth Lee Harris, December 17, 1780. Joseph Shelton, surety. Consent of her father, William Harris.

Coleman, Littleberry, and Milley Clark, spinster, September 29, 1800. William Tucker, surety. Nancy Coleman made oath that Milley Clark was left with her by Molly Bailey "when the said Bailey deceased about five years ago," and believes that Milley Clark was at that time about fourteen or fifteen years of age.

Coleman, Samuel, bachelor, and Judy Childress, spinster, February 26, 1794. Jesse Childress, surety. Consent of Joseph Childress.

Coleman, Thomas, bachelor, and Anne Coleman, spinster, October 2, 1786. Thomas Lucas, surety. Consent of Million Coleman.

Collohon, Thomas, and Elizabeth ———. Certificate of marriage by the Rev. William Dameron, February 16, 1795. (M.R.) No M.L.B.

Conduitt, John, bachelor, and Polly Landrum, ———, 1794 (all the date given). Young Landrum, surety.

Connor, Daniel, and Elizabeth Bryant, widow, September 26, 1787. Parmenas Bryant, surety. Consent of Elizabeth, who states she is of age.

Connor, Jeremiah, and Elizabeth Tunget, February 19, 1796. Dennis Mahony, surety, who made oath that Elizabeth was of age.

Cook, William, bachelor, and Liddey Bailey, spinster, daughter of John Bailey, January 8, 1781. John Bailey, surety.

Cooper, Joseph, bachelor, of Henry County, and Jane Dillard, spinster, September 8, 1788. Drury Bell, surety. Consent of his father, Thomas Cooper. Consent of her father, James Dillard.

Cooper, Robert, and Martha Thompson, spinster, August 10, 1799. John Thompson, surety. Consent of James Thompson, Sr. Certificate of marriage by the Rev. James Boyd. (M.R.)

Copeland, Martin, bachelor, and Nancy Lobban, December 21, 1795. John McCarter, surety. Consent of her father, James Lobban.

Coulter, John, and Frances Johnson, spinster, April 25, 1795. William S. Crawford, surety. (Bond is not signed.)

Coulter, Michael, and Frances Johnson, April 25, 1795. William S. Crawford, surety. Certificate of marriage by the Rev. Charles Crawford. (M.R.)

Couney, John, bachelor, and Milley Edmonds, spinster, June 27, 1789. Samuel Edmonds, surety. Consent of her father, James Edmonds.

Courtney, Samuel, and Nancy Baddow, spinster, September 7, 1797. Vincent Packett, surety. Consent of her father, Thomas *Beddow,* for her to marry Samuel *Cortneys,* of Buckingham Co. See: *"Samuel Coatney."*

Cox, Archelaus, and Mary Ann Hughs, spinster, June 15, 1773. Joseph Tucker, surety.

Cox, Edward, and Margaret Higginbotham, spinster, December 14, 1778. Wm. Oglesby, surety. Consent of [her father], Aaron Higginbotham, Sr.

Cox, Milliner, bachelor, and Sally Bolling, spinster, March 13, 1797. James Bolling, surety.

Cox, Vollintine, and Nancy Dawson, spinster, March 3, 1772. Gabriel Penn, surety.

Crank, Thomas, bachelor, and Mary Carpenter, spinster, December 15, 1794. James Carpenter, surety. Consent of her mother, Sarah Carpenter, widow. Certificate of marriage by the Rev. Ezekial Campbell. (M.R.)

Crawford, John, bachelor, and Mary Ann Burrus, spinster, December 6, 1784. Charles Taliaferro, Jr., surety. Consent of Charles Burrus as to Mary Ann Burrus.

Crawford, John Dennis, bachelor, and Rebeckah Staton, spinster, December 4, 1786. John Smith, surety. Consent of Ann Staton.

Crawford, Nelson, bachelor, and Lucy Crawford, spinster, April 15, 1793. Consent of her father, Nathan Crawford.
Note. The above bond apparently refers to the parties married by the Rev. Mr. Crawford, 1793, and recorded by him as follows: "Marriages by Rev. Mr. Crawford—1793. Crawford with Crawford." (M.R.)

Crawford, William Sid. (William Sidney Crawford), bachelor, and Sophia Penn, spinster, November 16, 1785. James Callaway, surety. Consent of her father, Gabriel Penn.

Crews, Lewis, bachelor, and Nancy Taylor, spinster, April 30, 1796. James Ham, surety, who made oath that Nancy was 21 years of age. Consent of her father, Charles Taylor.

Crews, Reuben P., and Charlotte Crews, May 13, 1797. Joseph Crews, surety, who made oath that Reuben Pettijohn Crews was 21 years of age.

Crews, Wrenney, bachelor, of Campbell County, and Judith Hughes, spinster, December 30, 1789. Harrison Hughes, surety. Consent of her father, William Hughes.

Crisp, John, and Milley Alford, spinster, December 16, 1799. John Camm, surety. Consent of William Crisp and William Alford. Certificate of marriage by the Rev. James Boyd. (M.R.)

Crutcher, William, and Elizabeth Pollard. Certificate of marriage by the Rev. Joseph Ballinger, January 16, 1784. (Order Book 1782-1784, p. 210.)

Dakin, Jonathan, bachelor, and Sally Crews, spinster, December 3, 1787. Zachariah Dawson, surety. Consent of her father, James Crews.

Dameron, William, bachelor, and Susanna Lee, widow, March 23, 1787. Joshua Shelton, surety. Consent of Susanna.

Darnell, Isaac, bachelor, and Elizabeth Diggs, spinster, December 7, 1789. Charles Crawford, surety. Consent of her father, John Diggs.

Davenport, Richard, and Mary Christian, were married by the Rev. William McKendrie, September 1, 1796. (M.R.)

Davenport, William, bachelor, and Elizabeth Wingfield, spinster, January 3, 1791. Peter Joyner, surety. Consent of his father, Joseph Davenport. Consent of her father, Nathan Wingfield.

Davenport, William, bachelor, and Mary Christian, spinster, August 31, 1796. John Christian, surety.

Davies, Henry Landon, widower, and Lucy Whiting Manson, widow, August 15, 1786. Charles Taliaferro, Jr., surety. Consent of Lucy Whiting Manson.

Davies, Nicholas, bachelor, and Elizabeth Crawford, spinster, October 13, 1789. Nathaniel Crawford, Jr., surety. Consent of his father, Henry L. Davies for his son, Nicholas Clayton Davies to apply for a license to marry Miss Elizabeth Crawford, daughter of Captain David Crawford. Consent of her father, David Crawford, she being under age.

Davis, Charles, bachelor, and Rosannah Ellis, spinster, July 1, 1782. Jonah Ellis, surety. Consent of Rosannah. Jonah Ellis certified that Rosannah was of lawful age. Certificate of marriage by the Rev. Charles Clay, July 4, 1782. (Order Book, 1782-1784, p. 107.)

Davis, Davis, bachelor, and Fanny Bolling, spinster, November 13, 1793. William Davis, surety. Consent of Elizabeth Davis. William Davis made oath that Fanny Bolling was 21 years of age. Certificate of marriage by the Rev. Ezekiel Campbell, 1794. (M.R.)

Davis, Edmund, widower, and Milly Fitzgerald, spinster, September 3, 1793. James Fitzgerald, surety. Consent of her father, James Fitzgerald.

Davis, George, bachelor, and Nancy Taylor, spinster, January 15, 1791. George Taylor, surety.

Davis, George, and Nancy Taylor, January 12, 1790. Consent of David Davis and William Taylor. This is a consent only.

Davis, Jabus, bachelor, and Christian Allen, spinster, May 6, 1790. Philip Davis, surety. Consent of his mother, Hannah Davis. Consent of her father, Joseph Allen.

Davis, James, bachelor, and Martha Reid, spinster, January 1, 1785. Jonathan Reid, surety. Consent of her father, Alexander Reid.

Davis, Joel, and Sally Bethel, spinster, December 23, 1792. John Davis, surety. Consent of her father, John Bethel.

Davis, John, and Margaret Hardy. Certificate of marriage by the Rev. Benjamin Berger, 1782. Returned at a court held August 5, 1782. (Order Book 1782-1784, p. 1.)

Davis, John, bachelor, and Margaret Burns, spinster, November 21, 1792. Lewis Davis, surety. Consent of Margaret. Lewis Davis made oath that Margaret was upwards of 21 years of age. Certificate of marriage by the Rev. Mr. Campbell, 1793. (M.R.)

Davis, Larkin, bachelor, and Salley Carter, spinster, October 25, 1785. Richard Lawless, surety. Consent of his father, Richard Davis. Consent of her father, Solomon Carter.

Davis, Lewis, and Elizabeth Bugg, March 9, 1797. Sherod Bugg, surety.

Davis, Moses, bachelor, and Millicent Carter, spinster, daughter of Solomon Carter, November 19, 1779. John Ware, surety. Consent of her parents, Solomon and Mary Carter.

Davis, Philip, bachelor, and Sarah Thompson, spinster, April 22, 1794. John Thompson, surety. Certificate of marriage by the Rev. Ezekiel Campbell. (M.R.)

Davis, William, bachelor, and Elizabeth Goode, spinster, March 28, 1789. David Davis, surety. Consent of her father, Daniel Goode.

Davis, William, bachelor, and Benedicter Milsted, spinster, January 1, 1787. Peter Carter, surety. Consent of Joseph Milsted.

Davis, William, bachelor, and Frances Green, spinster, April 20, 1786. John Davis, surety. Consent of Frances.

Dawson, Jesse, bachelor, and Salley Turner, spinster, December 15, 1791. James Tinsley, surety. Consent of her father, Henry Turner. Consent of Salley.

Dawson, John Sorrell, bachelor, and Jane Lyon, spinster, February 11, 1786. Benjamin Dawson, surety. Consent of her father, Peter Lyon.

Dawson, Martin, bachelor, and Milly Cox, spinster, October 18, 1795. Zach Dawson, surety. Certificate of marriage by the Rev. Lewis Dawson. (M.R.)

Dawson, Pleasant, bachelor, and Sary Turner, spinster, February 6, 1786. John Sorrell Dawson, surety. Consent of her father, James Turner, who calls her "Sarah."

Dawson, Pleasant, bachelor, and Sarah Christian, spinster, March 7, 1791. John Christian, surety. Consent of her mother, Elizabeth Christian.

Dawson, Zachariah, bachelor, and Lucy Rucker, spinster, January 18, 1786. James Franklin, surety. Consent of her father, Benjamin Rucker.

Dehart, Jesse, and Jemima Wood, spinster, November 4, 1800. Paul Wood, surety, who made oath that Jesse Dehart was over 21 years of age.

Dehart, John, bachelor, and Eleander Scott, spinster, September 3, 1792. Benjamin Plunkett, surety. Consent of Eleander, "of lawful age." Consent of Aaron Dehart.

Demasters, Edward, bachelor, and Sally Carter, spinster, August 20, 1794. William Clarkson, surety. Consent of her father, Thomas Carter. Certificate of marriage by the Rev. Ezekiel Campbell. (M.R.)

Dempsey, William, and Patsey Landrum, spinster, August 21, 1799. Allen Cameron, surety. Consent of her mother, Susannah Dempsey. Certificate of marriage by the Rev. James Boyd. (M.R.)

Dennis, Elisha, bachelor, and Elizabeth Hudson, spinster, December 13, 1780. Robert Henderson, surety. Consent of her father, Joshua Hudson.

Dennis, Jesse, bachelor, and Rebecca Trail, spinster, October 20, 1794. Ashford Trail, surety. Consent of Rebecca (she calls herself "Rebe"). Ashford Trail made oath that Rebecca was over 21 years of age.

Depp, William, bachelor, of Powhatan County, and Elizabeth Walker, September 4, 1789. Joel Walker, surety.

Densmore, James, bachelor, and Sarah Phillips, spinster, April 15, 1793. John Masters, surety. Consent of her father, Thomas Phillips.

Densmore, William, bachelor, and Elizabeth Oglesby, spinster, May 21, 1792. Thomas Brady, surety. Consent of her mother, Easter Oglesby. Certificate of marriage by the Rev. Mr. Campbell, 1793. (M.R.)

Depriest, John, bachelor, and Ruth Campbell, spinster, September 19, 1791. George Campbell, surety. Consent of her mother, Margaret Henderson. Consent of Ruth.

Dibrell, Anthony, bachelor, and Wilmath Watson, spinster, November 3, 1790. James Watson, surety.

Dickinson, Thomas S., bachelor, and Susannah Rice Baker, spinster, August 26, 1795. Josias Baker, surety. Consent of her father, Josias Baker. Certificate of marriage by the Rev. Charles Crawford. (M.R.)

Dillard, George, bachelor, and Elizabeth Penn, spinster, October 2, 1792. James Ballinger, surety. Consent of her father, John Penn. Certificate of marriage by the Rev. Mr. Crawford. (M.R.)

Dillard, John, bachelor, and Sally Penn, spinster, September 17, 1791. Charles Watts, surety. Consent of her father, John Penn.

Dillard, John, and Sarah Stovall, spinster, December 23, 1771. Edmund Wilcox, surety. Consent of her father, George Stovall.

Dillard, Joseph, bachelor, and Judith Higginbotham, spinster, January 23, 1797. Reuben Crawford, surety. Consent of her father, James Higginbotham. Certificate of marriage by the Rev. Charles Crawford. (M.R.)

Dinsmore, Thomas, and Patsey Oglesby, spinster, July 27, 1790. William Forbes, surety. Consent of his mother, Mary Dinsmore, widow. Consent of her mother, Easter Oglesby. Certificate of marriage by the Rev. William Crawford. (M.R.)

Dinwiddie, John, bachelor, and Sarah Martin, widow, January 1, 1787. David Simpson, surety. Consent of Sarah.

Dinwiddie, Robert, bachelor, and Ann Barnett, spinster, November 29, 1788. Nathan Barnett, surety. Consent of her father, William Barnett.

Dinwiddie, William, bachelor, and Agnes Simpson, spinster, July 4, 1787. James Morrison, surety. Consent of her mother, Agnes Simpson, Sr.

Dodd, John, and Mary Carter, spinster, October 16, 1797. Joseph Dodd, surety. Consent of Frances Carter. Certificate of marriage by the Rev. Charles Crawford. (M.R.)

Dold, William, and Sally Brent, married by the Rev. William Crawford, 1798. (M.R.)

Donald, Andrew, of Bedford County, and Sally Moore, daughter of Benjamin Moore, deceased, November 18, 1794. Thomas Moore, surety.

Douglas, George, and Mary Tucker, spinster, April 13, 1769. Matthew Tucker, surety. Consent of her father, Drury Tucker.

Drummond, Henley, of James City County, and Agness Parson, spinster, March 3, 1783. Nathaniel Clark, surety.

Drummond, Henley, widower, and Mary Boutwell Taliaferro, spinster, January 19, 1789. David S. Garland, surety.

Duggens, Alexander, Jr., bachelor, and Salley Smith, spinster, January 22, 1788. David Duggens, surety. Consent of her mother, Ann Shoemaker.

Duggins, David, bachelor, and Lucy Stinnett, spinster, January 9, 1789. Skelton Napier, surety. Consent of William Stinnett.

Duggins, William, and Mary Goolsby, married by the Rev. Benjamin Coleman, March 1, 1784. (Order Book 1782-1784, p. 275.)

Duiguid, William, and Lucy Patteson, spinster, January 23, 1773. James Patteson, surety. Consent of her mother, Mary Patteson.

Duncan, Fleming, and Sally Johns, October 17, 1795. John Richer-

son, surety. Consent of John Richerson, guardian of Sally, who
stated that Fleming was 21 years of age. Certificate of marriage
by the Rev. Charles Crawford. (M.R.)

Duncan, William, and Sally Henley, spinster, March 26, 1798. John
Duncan, surety. Consent of Leonard Henley.

Durham, Isaac, and Judith Oglesby, spinster, January 23, 1798. William Forbes, surety, who made oath that Isaac Durham was 21
years of age. Consent of her mother, Easter Oglesby, widow.
Certificate of marriage by the Rev. William Crawford. (M.R.)

Durham, James, bachelor, and Caty Fitzgerald, spinster, October 28,
1793. Bartlett Fitzgerald, surety. Consent of his father, Thomas
Durham. Consent of her mother, Mary Durham. Patrick Fitzgerald made oath that Caty Fitzgerald (his sister) was 21 years
of age.

Durrett, Marshall, and Dorothy Woodroof, February 8, 1800. William
H. Digges, surety.

Eads, Bartlett, and Ann Rucker, April 12, 1795. James Ballinger,
surety. Consent of her father, Anthony Rucker. Bartlett Eads
made oath that Ann was 21 years of age.

Eads, Charles, bachelor, and Sarah Bowler, spinster, August 3, 1782.
John Wright, surety. Consent of William and Elizabeth Horrall,
parents-in-law of Sarah. Consent of Sarah.

Eads, Isaac, widower, and Sarah Bibie, widow, September 23, 1799.
John Campbell, surety.

Eads, William, and Jane W. Depriest, July 17, 1798. Martin Bryant,
surety. Consent of her mother, Amy Depriest, who calls her Jane
Walker Depriest, for her to marry William Eads, "orphan of John
Eads, deceased." Consent of John Staples as to William Eads.
Certificate of marriage by the Rev. William Crawford. (M.R.)

Eammes, Jonathan, bachelor, and Rosanna Swiney, widow, June 20,
1788. Caleb Higginbotham, surety. "To all People, This may
Certify that I Rosanna Swiney of Amherst County and State of
Virginia, have consented, and do desire, Reverently, discreately,
advisably, soberly & in the fear of God to be joined in holy Matri-
mony with Mr. Jona. Eammes of said County & State aforesaid—
Witness my hand.
Amherst County June 21st 1788.   Rosanna Swiney.
Test. Hendrick Arnold, Ruth Arnold.. To the Clerk of Amherst
County."

Edmonds, James, widower, and Mary Wooddy, widow, July 16, 1791.
Andrew Wright, surety. Consent of Mary.

Edmonds, John, bachelor, and Sally Wright, spinster, September 1,
1796. Austin Wright, surety, who made oath that Sally Wright
(his sister) was 21 years of age. Consent of her mother, Salley
Wright.

Edmonds, Rowland, bachelor, and Elizabeth Nevil, spinster, January 15, 1789. James Hansbrough, surety. "James Mathews produced a prayer book wherein the ages of several of the children of James Nevil, decd. is wrote in, wherein it appears that Elizabeth Nevil Daughter of the sd James Nevil Decd. was born on the 17th day of Sept. 1767 & he believes the handwriting is that of the sd James Nevil Decd. Sworn to before W. Cabell, Jan. 15, 1789."

Edmonds, Samuel, and Alse Wright, widow, September 22, 1777. Charles Irving, surety. Consent of Alse.

Edmonds, William, bachelor, and Sally Hughes, spinster, February 2, 1789. Moses Hughes, surety.

Edmunds, James, Jr., and Jean Innis, February 24, 1796. John Innis, surety. William Edmonds made oath that James was 21 years of age. James Edmunds, Jr., signed as *James Edmonds, Jr.*

Edmundson, John, Esq., and Ann Wiatt, spinster, February 26, 1771. Edmund Wilcox, surety. Consent of her father, Thomas Wiatt.

Edwards, Robert, and Sally Martin, December 16, 1800. Joseph Martin, surety. Consent of her father, Sherod Martin.

Edwards, Thomas, widower, and Nancy Hutcherson, spinster, October 2, 1786. John McDaniel, surety.

Edwards, Thomas, and Winney McDaniel, January 6, 1781. Consent of her father, George McDaniel. This is a consent only, there is no M. L. B.

Elgan, John, and Sally R. Wood, June 1, 1795. Silas Wood, surety. Consent of her father (not named).

Ellis, Charles, and Sarah Tucker, spinster. Not dated. Joseph Tucker, surety. Consent of her father, Matthew Tucker, August 25, 1770.

England, John, bachelor, and Mary Parsons, spinster, February 22, 1786. John Parsons, surety. Consent of his father, William England. Consent of her father, John Parsons.

England, William, and Jane Angus, January 31, 1799. William Angus, surety.

Enix, David, Jr., bachelor, and Sally Lannum, spinster, October 20, 1789. John Jopling, surety. Consent of her parents, Benedick and Nelley Lannum.

Ennis, George, bachelor, and Frances Campbell, spinster, December 24, 1796. Ambrose Campbell, surety. Certificate of marriage by the Rev. William Crawford. (M.R.)

Evans, Charles, and Elizabeth Wright, October 11, 1797. Menos Wright, surety. Certificate of marriage by the Rev. Walter Christion. (M.R.)

Evans, Charles, bachelor, and Elcy Purvis, spinster, May 13, 1791. Charles Purvis, surety. Consent of her father, George Purvis.

Evans, George, bachelor,, and Pattey Gatewood, spinster, October 6, 1789. Henry Gatewood, surety. Consent of William *Evins* and Richard Gatewood.

Evans, James, bachelor, and Ann Pamplin, spinster, January 21, 1796. James Pamplin, surety. Consent of her father, James Pamplin. James Pamplin (Ann's brother) made oath that she was 21 years of age.

Evans, Robert, and Martha England, September 2, 1795. William Angus, surety. Consent of his father, William Evans.

Evans, Thomas, bachelor, and Anna Penn, November 2, 1795. John Lonagan, surety. Consent of her father, Rolly Penn.

Ewers, William, and Polly Barnett, spinster, August 7, 1797. John Barnett, surety. Consent of her father, William Barnett. Certificate of marriage by the Rev. William Crawford. (M.R.)

Farguson, Samuel, bachelor, and Susannah Ball, spinster, September 4, 1793. David Farguson, surety. Consent of her father, William Ball. Consent of Susannah.

Farnsworth, Henry, of Campbell County, and Damaris Cox, spinster, October 16, 1799. Samuel Burks, surety. Consent of her father, Volentine Cox. (1799.)

Farrar, John, bachelor, and Mary Morrison, widow, January 1, 1788. George Morris, surety. Consent of Mary.

Felix, John, and Sally Haynes, married by the Rev. Mr. Crawford, 1793. (M.R.) See *Philiere*. Felix, however, is correct.
John Philiere and Sally Haynes, ——— 4, 1793. Jesse Haynes, surety. Bond is signed *John Felix*. Bond is endorsed *Philere & Haynes*. Consent of her father, William Haynes.

Fendley, Andrew, bachelor, and Sarah Nally, spinster, May 16, 1785. William Nally, surety.

Fenton, Zachariah, and Sophia Bryant, spinster, November 17, 1798. William Bryant, surety. Certificate of marriage by the Rev. Walter Christian. (M.R.)

Fidler, Jesse, bachelor, and Rhoda Enix, spinster, August 18, 1794. Nathaniel Wade, surety. Consent of David and Sary *Enicks* for *Jessey Fielden* to obtain a marriage license to wed *Roady Enicks*.

Finch, John, bachelor, and Edey Wood, spinster, August 25, 1787. Orson Knight, surety. Consent of her father, Robert Wood.

Fitzgarrell, Hugh, and Sarah Smith, spinster, May 25, 1799. William Smith, surety, who made oath that Sarah was over 21 years of age. Consent of her father, Andrew Smith. Certificate of marriage by the Rev. Walter Christian, May 27, 1799. (M.R.)

Fitzhugh, Thomas, and Ann Rose, spinster, January 4, 1778. Patrick Rose and Edmund Wilcox, sureties. Consent of her father, John Rose, who calls her "Anne Rose," and consents to her marriage to "Thomas Fitzhugh, of Stafford County."

Fitzpatrick, Samuel, and Ann Sparks, June 18, 1792. Dennet Witt, surety. Consent of her father, David Witt.

Fitzpatrick, Thomas, bachelor, and Lydia Cartwright, spinster, October 21, 1793. Joseph Roberts, surety, who stated that Lydia was over 21 years of age.

Fitzpatrick, Thomas, and Elizabeth Witt, spinster, November 22, 1798. James McClain, surety. Consent of her mother, Jean Witt.

Flood, John, and Martha Carter, spinster, September 12, 1800. Abram Carter, surety.

Flora, Peter, bachelor, and Elizabeth Brown, spinster, April 3, 1786. Robert Hudson, surety. Consent of her mother, Rachel Brown.

Floyd, Charles, bachelor, and Mary Stewart, spinster, July 3, 1786. Charles Stewart, surety. Consent of Mary, who stated she was of lawful age.

Forbes, Alexander, bachelor, and Catherine Clifton, spinster, September 13, 1787. James McAlexander, surety. Consent of Catherine.

Forbes, Angus, and Mary Lee, were married by the Rev. W. Irvine, November 20, 1780. (Order Book 1773-1782, p. 511.)

Ford, Abner, and Elizabeth Dawson, spinster, December 4, 1798. Martin Dawson, Sr., surety. Consent of her father, John Dawson, for her to marry "Abner Ford, of the County of Charlotte."

Fortune, Eddy, bachelor, and Becky Ponton, spinster, December 21, 1791. John Fortune, surety. Consent of Thomas Fortune.

Fortune, Jesse, and Betsy Lavender, July 15, 1793. Jesse Mills, surety. Consent of his parents, Thomas and Elizabeth Fortune. Consent of her mother, Milley Walton. Certificate of marriage by the Rev. William Dawson, July 22, 1793. (M.R.)

Fortune, Richard, bachelor, and Mary Lavender, spinster, September 4, 1786. Charles Lavender, surety. Consent of her mother, Milley Lavender.

Fortune, Williamson, bachelor, son of John Fortune, of Albemarle County, and Sarah Henderson, spinster, daughter of William Henderson, Jr., of Amherst County, January 26, 1780. William Henderson, Jr., surety.

"Jany. 25th, 1780. Then Benjamin Fortune made Oath before me, that his brother Williamson Fortune, was born into this life, on the 4th day of December 1758 as he believes, from the following reasons: He the sd Benjamin having seen the day and date that the sd Williamson was born on Wrote by the father of the above sd in a prayer book belonging to the sd father, and hath repeatedly heard the sd father say that the sd Williamson was his own man.

Zachs. Talliaferro."

Fortune, Zacharias, bachelor, and Betsey Burnett, spinster, January 5, 1789. John Fortune, surety. Consent of her father, John Burnett.

Foster, James, bachelor, and Nancy Shepherd, December 27, 1785. John Clarkson, surety. Consent of her father, Augustine Shepherd.

Foster, William, bachelor, and Mary Bethel, August 19, 1793. Joseph
Lively, Jr., surety. Consent of her father, John Bethel.

Fowler, James, bachelor, and Jenny Hilley, spinster, September 3,
1788. Nelson Carter Dawson, surety. Consent of Jenny. Benjamin Rucker testified she was 21 years of age.

Fox, John, and Lucy Mathews, spinster, February 17, 1800. George
Ozburn, surety.

Fox, Joseph, bachelor, and Susannah Smith, spinster, October 24,
1791. Samuel Smith, surety. Consent of Joseph Smith.

Franklin, James, bachelor, and Nancy Crews, spinster, December 15,
1796. Reuben Crawford, surety. Certificate of marriage by the
Rev. William Crawford. (M.R.)

Franklin, Jasper, bachelor, and Polly Brockman, spinster, October 27,
1796. Reubin Franklin, surety. Consent of her mother, Elizabeth
Brockman.

Franklin, Peachy, and Susannah Dillard, spinster, March 20, 1799.
Spotswood Garland, surety.

Franklin, Reubin, bachelor, and Matilda Harrison, spinster, November
2, 1796. Reubin Harrison, surety.

Franklin, Samuel, bachelor, and Rachel Powell, spinster, January 1,
1794. James Ballinger, surety. Consent of her father, Thomas
Powell.

Frazier, John (he signed his name "John Fraser") and Dolly Higgin-
botham, spinster, December 14, 1799. Edward Vickers, surety.
Consent of her father, William Higginbotham. Certificate of Rev.
John Young that he married them December 17, 1799.

Fulcher, George, and Fanny Penn, married April 15, 1783, by the
Rev. Joseph Ballinger. (Order Book 1782-1784, p. 121.)

Fulcher, James, bachelor, and Salley Faris, spinster, October 12, 1793.
William Fulcher, surety. Consent of George Gillespie and Mary
Gillespie. Certificate of marriage by the Rev. Mr. Crawford.
(M.R.)

Fulcher, John, bachelor, and Elizabeth Huckstep, spinster, January 4,
1788. Richard Fulcher, surety. Consent of her parents, Samuel
and Anne Huckstep.

Gabhart, Peter, of Rockbridge County, and Sally Coleman, March 1,
1793. John Reid, surety. Consent of Ben Coleman. Certificate of
marriage by the Rev. Mr. Houston, of Rockbridge, December 6,
1794. (M.R.)

Gahagan, James, bachelor, and Elizabeth Murrill, spinster, January
15, 1798 (date of consent). John *Murrell,* surety. Consent of
John Murrill.

Gahagan, James, and Sarah Binnian, spinster, December 2, 1799.
Joseph Murrell, surety. Jesse Murrell made oath that Sarah
Binnian, daughter of Martin Binnian, was 21 years old. Cer-
tificate of marriage by the Rev. William Crawford. (M.R.)

Gaines, Daniel, Gent., and Miss Mary Gilbert, October 6, 1777. Edmund Wilcox, surety. Consent of her father, Henry Gilbert.

Galespy, Sherred Moore, bachelor, and Sally Horsley, spinster, February 12, 1778. John Thurmond and Roland Horsley sureties. Consent of Sally.

Garland, David S., bachelor, and Jane Meredith, spinster, March 4, 1795. Reuben Crawford, surety. Consent of her father, Samuel Meredith, who calls her "Jane H. Meredith." Certificate of marriage by the Rev. Charles Crawford. (M.R.)

Garland, Hudson, bachelor, and Elizabeth Phillips, spinster, August 19, 1791. William Allcock, surety. Consent of his guardian, Charles Wingfield. Consent of her father, John Phillips.

Garland, Nathaniel, and Jane Rodes, spinster, December 7, 1772. Edmund Wilcox, surety. Consent of her father, Charles Rodes, "she not being of lawful age."

Garland, Spotswood, and Polly Stone, spinster, September 8, 1800. Henry Woods, surety. Consent of her father, B. Stone.

Gatewood, Henry, bachelor, and Oliva Rains, spinster, April 3, 1786. Walter Christian, surety. Consent of his father, Richard Gatewood for his son, Richard to marry "Olivia Rains, daughter of Nancy Rains."

Gatewood, James, bachelor, and Elizabeth Shoemaker, spinster, July 6, 1789. Joseph Lively, surety. Consent of Elizabeth Shoemaker for James Gatewood to marry her daughter, *Sarah* Shoemaker.

Gatewood, Ramson, and Elizabeth Burks, spinster, November 9, 1799. William Parks, surety. Consent of her father, Charles Burks.

Gentry, James, bachelor, and Elizabeth Lyon, spinster, March 10, 1788. Benjamin Childress, surety. Consent of her father, William Lyon.

Gibson, Jacob, bachelor, and Jane Tyree, spinster, March 28, 1791. Jacob Tyree, surety.

Gilbert, Ezekiel, bachelor, and Ann Rukins Bryan, spinster, March 6, 1781. Ambrose Rucker, surety.

Gilbert, Ezekiel, and Mary Dunnavin (alias Gilbert), January 27, 1800. Henry Gilbert, surety, who made oath that Mary Dunnavin (alias Gilbert) was 21 years of age. Certificate of marriage by the Rev. W. Christian. (M.R.)

Gilbert, George, and Miss Martha Cole West, spinster, March 7, 1783. Daniel Gaines, Gent., surety. John Stewart, aged 53 years, deposes that to his certain knowledge Miss Martha Cole West, daughter of John West, Esqr., is over the age of 21 years. Martha Cole West deposes, March 5, 1783, that she was 21 or 22 years of age June last past from a register kept by her father. Certificate of marriage by the Rev. Charles Clay, March 7, 1783. (Order Book 1782-1784, p. 107.)

Giles, James, bachelor, and Jemimah T. Coffey, December 19, 1797. Richard Taliaferro, surety. Consent of Winneyford Hays and

Thomas Hays. Certificate of marriage by the Rev. William Crawford. (M.R.)

Giles, William, and Peggy Martin, September 29, 1797, Samuel Martin, surety. Consent of Moses Martin, half-brother of Peggy, who states that she "is going on 21 years." James Martin made oath that Peggy was 21 years of age.

Gillaspie, Lewis, and Betsy Farris, spinster, February 4, 1800. George Gillaspie, surety.

Gillespie, George, Jr., bachelor, and Mary Faris, spinster, June 7, 1790. George Gillespie, surety.

Gillespie, William, and Ann Hudson, spinster, December 23, 1777. Joshua Hudson and Edmund Wilcox, sureties.

Gilliam, James, bachelor, and Susanna Penn, spinster, August 18, 1794. Randolph Profitt, surety. Consent of her step-father and mother, John and Ann Savage.

Gillinwaters, Joshua, and Sally Layne, December 21, 1797. William Layne, Jr., surety, who made oath that Sally Layne, daughter of James Layne, was 21 years of age. Certificate of marriage by Rev. Walter Christian.

Gleeson, Thomas, bachelor, and Judy Stone, spinster, April 2, 1788. Marble Stone, surety.

Goff, William, and Betsey Whitten, were married by the Rev. Benjamin Coleman, January 8, 1784. (Order Book 1782-1784, p. 210.)

Gooch, Philip, widower, and Frances Phillips, spinster, December 22, 1790. John Loving, Jr., surety. Consent of her father, William Phillips.

Goode, Daniel C., bachelor, and Mary Bryant, widow, January 17, 1797. William Wortham, surety. Consent of Mary.

Goode, William, and Mary Wortham, spinster, November 27, 1797. Nolley Wortham, surety. Consent of her father, George Wortham. Sherwood (Sherrod) Bugg made oath that William Goode was 21 years of age. Certificate of marriage by Rev. Charles Crawford. (M.R.)

Goodrich, James, widower, and Jane Brown, spinster, August 22, 1789. John Peyton, surety. Consent of her mother, Susanna Brown.

Goodrich, John, bachelor, and Mary Carter, widow, September 20, 1786. John Campbell, surety. John and Mary give their consent and state they are of lawful age.

Goodrich, Samuel, bachelor, and Elizabeth Walton, spinster, December 25, 1789. Landon Carter, surety. Consent of his father, James Goodrich. Consent of her father, William Walton, for her to marry Samuel Eliot Goodrich.

Goodwin, John Henry, bachelor, and Mary Johnson, daughter of Jonathan Johnson, July 9, 1779. Charles Burrass, surety. Consent of his father, John Goodwin for him to marry Mary Johnson, daughter of "Jonathan Johnson, deceased." Anne

Johnson testifies that her daughter Mary Johnson, is 20 year
of age.

Goodwin, Warner, and Esther Camden, spinster, January 31, 180
William Camden, surety.

Goolsbey, James, and Nancy Matthews, married by the Rev. Ben
jamin Coleman, April 18, 1782. (Order Book 1773-1782, p. 511.

Goolsby, Samuel, bachelor, and Ephey Marr, spinster, April 5, 178
John Marr, Jr., surety. Consent of her father, John Marr.

Graves, Richard, and Milley Murrill, March 14, 1796. John Murril
surety.

Green, Greenberry, bachelor, and Abigaile Martain, spinster, No
vember 15, 1780. Henry Martin, surety.

Gregory, John, and Elizabeth Turner, spinster, December 7, 179!
Teresha Turner, surety. Consent of her father, Henry Turne

Gregory, Thomas, and Polly London, spinster, December 19, 179!
John London, surety. Consent of her father, James London

Gresham, Thomas, Jr., and Nancy Sledd, May 8, 1797. Rober
Gresham, surety. Consent of his father, Thomas *Grissham*. Cer
tificate of marriage by Rev. Charles Crawford, who calls hir
Thomas *Grissom*. (M.R.)

Gresham, Thomas, bachelor, and Maryann Dillard, spinster, Octobe
9, 1787. Drury Bell, surety. Consent of her father, James Di
lard. Consent of Maryann.

Grey, Isaac, and Betsy Small. On list of "Marriages by Rev. Willia
Crawford, 1796-1797." "The last couple published agreeable
law." (M.R.)

Griffin, Charles, bachelor, and Nancy Griffin, spinster, December 1!
1791. Thomas Griffin, surety.

Griffin, John, bachelor, and Ann Wortham, spinster, August 3, 178!
James Stevens, Jr., surety. Consent of her father, Thoma
Wortham.

Griffin, John Merry, widower, and Esther Wright, spinster, Novembe
14, 1792. Samuel Spencer, surety. Consent of John Merry Gri
fin. Consent of her father, Robert Wright, Sr.

Griffin, Lindsay, and Sally Hare, spinster, October 2, 1797. Benjami
Childress, surety. Consent of her father, Richard Hare.

Griffin, William, bachelor, and Authorie Griffin, spinster, Februar
10, 1789. Thomas Griffin, surety.

Griffin, William, bachelor, and Ruth Lively, June 17, 1793. Ezeki
Hill, surety. Consent of her father, Joseph Lively. Certificat
of marriage by Rev. Mr. Crawford. (M.R.)

Griffith, Thomas, bachelor, and Mary Jones, spinster, February
1794. Bartholomew Staton, surety. Consent of Mary, who state
she was 25 years of age.

Groome, John, bachelor, and Catherine Riggins, widow, December
1783. Peter Carter, surety. Consent of Catherine. Certificate

marriage by Rev. Benjamin Coleman, December 6, 1783. (Order Book 1782-1784, p. 210.)

Gue, John, and Peggy Whitten, married by the Rev. Benjamin Coleman, April 9, 1782. (Order Book 1773-1782, p. 511.)

Guthry, William, and Elizabeth Wingfield, January 26, 1797. John Wingfield, surety.

Guttry, Nathaniel, bachelor, and Nancy Johns, spinster, February 7, 1790. John H. Goodwin, surety. Consent of her mother, Mary Johns.

Hacock, Abanezer, bachelor, and Jane Linn, widow, April 14, 1784. Thomas Watt, surety. Consent of Jane. Certificate of marriage by the Rev. Benjamin Coleman, April 27, 1784. (Order Book 1782-1784, p. 275.) See *Haycock*.

Haycock, Abanezer, and Jane Linn, married by the Rev. Benjamin Coleman, April 27, 1784. (Order Book 1782-1784, p. 275.) See *Hacock*.

Hail, Lenard, bachelor, and Elizabeth Hall, spinster, January 17, 1786. Elisha Witt, surety. Consent of her parents, John and Bette Hall.

Haines, Jesse, bachelor, and Milley Tinsley, spinster, November 4, 1793. Reubin Tinsley, surety. Consent of her father, William Tinsley.

Halbert, John, bachelor, and Sarah Steel, spinster, January 16, 1792. William Williams, surety. Consent of John Halbert and Sarah Steel. Certificate of marriage by the Rev. Mr. Coleman, January 22, 1792. (M.R.)

Ham, Ambrose, bachelor, and Tabitha Gatewood, spinster, October 5, 1790. Richard Gatewood, surety. Consent of Stephen Ham [father of Ambrose]. Consent of her father, Richard Gatewood. Consent of Tabitha.

Ham, James, bachelor, and Mourning Burford, spinster, December 18, 1787. John Ham, surety. Consent of his father, Stephen Ham. Consent of her father, John Burford.

Ham, James, and Nancey Crews, February 20, 1796. Lewis Crews, surety. Consent of her father, James Crews. Certificate of marriage by the Rev. Lewis Dawson. (M.R.)

Ham, John, bachelor [son of Stephen Ham], and Betsey Gatewood, spinster, December 18, 1787. James Ham, surety. Consent of her father, Richard Gatewood.

Hambleton, Andrew, bachelor, and Elizabeth Mays, spinster, November 2, 1795. William Hambleton, surety. Consent of Milley Hambleton. Certificate of marriage by the Rev. Charles Crawford. (M.R.)

Hambleton, Robert, bachelor, and Milley Mays, spinster, May 10, 1791. John Mays, surety.

Hamner, Morris, bachelor, of Albemarle County, and Mary Lucas, February 5, 1793. James Marr, surety. Consent of Mary. Certificate of marriage by the Rev. Mr. Crawford. (M.R.)

Hansard, William, bachelor, and Martha Christian, spinster, November 24, 1792. Robert Christian, surety. Consent of her mother, Mary Christian. Certificate of marriage by the Rev. Mr. Crawford. (M.R.)

Hansford, John, bachelor, and Caroline Rucker, spinster, November 23, 1793. Isaac Rucker, surety. Consent of her father, Ambrose Rucker. Bond is made out in the name of John Hansford, but he signed as John *Hansard*.

Harding, Edward, bachelor, and Agness Warwick, spinster, daughter of Abraham Warwick, June 7, 1779. Groves Harding, surety.

Harding, Edward, widower, and Mary Partree Burks, spinster, December 15, 1784. Bransford West, surety. Consent of her father, Samuel Burks.

Hardwick, Richard, bachelor, and Nancy Coleman, spinster, October 20, 1794. James Marr, surety. Consent of her mother, Elizabeth Coleman.

Hardy, Robert, bachelor, and Mary Bridgwater, spinster, January 9, 1790. John Davis, surety. Consent of her father, Jonathan Bridgwater.

Hare, William B., bachelor, and Elizabeth Cabell, spinster, July 4, 1793. Gideon Crews, surety. Consent of her father, N. Cabell. Certificate of marriage by the Rev. Mr. Crawford. (M.R.)

Hargrove, Hezekiah, and Susannah Murphy, widow, September 8, 1772. Joseph Dawson, surety. Consent of Susannah.

Harlow, Rowland, and Ann Henderson, spinster, March 2, 1799. Spotswood Garland, surety. Consent of his father, Nathaniel Harlow (who stated that Rowland was 24 years old), for him to marry Ann Henderson, "daughter of John Henderson." Consent of her parents, John and Margaret Henderson, who stated that she was 18 years of age.

Harlow, William and Patsey Ewers, spinster, September 1, 1798. William Ewers, surety. Consent of her father, Thomas Ewers. Certificate of marriage by the Rev. William Crawford. (M.R.)

Harris, Edward, bachelor, and Kitty Diggs, spinster, December 19, 1796. William Lee Harris, surety. Consent of her father, John *Digges*. Certificate of marriage by the Rev. William Crawford. (M.R.)

Harris, James, and Lucy Puckett, spinster, November 6, 1797. Jacob Puckett, surety. Certificate of marriage by the Rev. William Crawford. (M.R.)

Harris, Nathan, and Sarah Mosby, spinster, March 6, 1797. John Mosby, surety. Consent of her father, Daniel Mosby. Certificate of marriage by the Rev. William Crawford.

Harris, William, and Susanna Roberts, November 10, 1792. George Wharton, surety. Consent of Elizabeth Roberts. Consent of Susanna.

Harrison, Battail, bachelor, and Frances Tinsley, spinster, November 17, 1792. Edward Tinsley, surety. Consent of her father, John Tinsley. (He signed as "Battle Harrison.")

Harrison, James, bachelor, and Polly Penn, spinster, November 8, 1780. Samuel Camp, surety.

Harrison, Josiah, and Rachel A. Davis, spinster, December 24, 1800. Thomas Stewart, surety.

Harrison, Nicholas, and Nancy Hill, widow, April 18, 1800. Thomas Woodroof, surety. Consent of his father, Richard Harrison, who states that Nicholas is 21 years of age. Consent of her father, David Woodroof.

Harrison, Richard, Jr., bachelor, and Milley Tucker, spinster, December 27, 1788. Bennami Stone, surety. Consent of her father, Drury Tucker.

Hartless, Henry, and Jane Clarke, July 7, 1798. William Clark, surety.

Hartless, Peter, bachelor, and Jean Mason, spinster, January 2, 1792. Thomas Allen, surety. Consent of Thomas and Jane Mason.

Hartless, William, bachelor, and Nancy Staton, spinster, February 7, 1785. John Jarvis, surety. Consent of her mother, Ann Staton. Certificate of marriage by the Rev. Joseph Ballinger, February 14, 1785. (Order Book 1784-1787, p. 111.)

Harvie, Daniel, bachelor, and Sally Taliaferro, spinster, October 30, 1782. James Stevens, Jr., surety. Consent of her father, Zachs. Taliaferro. Certificate of marriage by the Rev. Charles Clay, November 1, 1782. (Order Book 1782-1784, p. 107.)

Harvie, Thomas, and Betsey Seay, October 19, 1795. Abraham Seay, surety. Certificate of marriage by the Rev. William Crawford. (M.R.)

Haskins, Thomas, bachelor, and Parmelia Penn, spinster, September 14, 1787. James Callaway, surety. Consent of her father, Gabriel Penn.

Haslip, Thomas, and Jane Lackland, married by the Rev. Benjamin Coleman, April 21, 1783. (Order Book 1782-1784, p. 111.)

Hawkins, John, and Patsey Martin, spinster, October 29, 1799. William H. Digges, surety. Consent of her father, Pleas. (Pleasant) Martin. Certificate of marriage by the Rev. William Crawford. (M.R.)

Hawkins, Thomas, and Elizabeth Powell, spinster, March 5, 1771. Edmund Wilcox, surety.

Haynes, Charles, bachelor, and Nancy Goodrich, spinster, January 1, 1786. George Galaspie, Jr., surety. Consent of William Haynes. Consent of her father, John Goodrich, who states that both she and Charles Haynes are of age.

Haynes, Jesse, and Milly Tinsley, married by the Rev. Mr. Crawford. No date, but the date preceding this list of Mr. Crawford's is 1793.

Haynes, Josiah, bachelor, and Judith New, spinster, April 28, 1794. Jesse Haynes, surety. Consent of his mother, Sarah Haynes. Consent of her mother, Elizabeth New.

Haynes, William, widower, and Sarah New, widow, December 13, 1793. Robert Holloway, surety. Consent of Sarah.

Hays, Thomas, and Winneford Coffin, March 28, 1792. Patrick Higgins, surety. William Coffy requests Clerk to issue a marriage license to Thomas Hays to marry Wineford *Coffy.* Certificate of marriage of Thomas Hays and Winifred Coffee, March 29, 1792, by Rev. Mr. Day. (M.R.)

Heard, John, bachelor, and Mary Montgomery, spinster, July 8, 1778. David Montgomery, Jr., surety, who made oath that Mary Montgomery (his sister) was 24 years old.

Henderson, Alexander, bachelor, and Sarah Dinwiddie, spinster, daughter of Robert Dinwiddie, May 25, 1779. Thomas Morrison, surety.

Henderson, Benjamin, and Mary Smith, spinster, January 7, 1784. Thomas Smith, surety. Consent of her father, Andrew Smith, Sr.

Henderson, John, and Sally Fortune, spinster, December 25, 1797. Benjamin Fortune, surety. Consent of Sally. Benjamin Fortune made oath that John Henderson was 21 years of age. Certificate of marriage by Rev. Walter Christian. (M.R.)

Henderson, Joseph, and Nancy Becknall, spinster, July 31, 1799. Alexander McAlexander, surety, who made oath that Joseph Henderson was 21 years of age. Consent of her mother, Lucy Becknall. Certificate of marriage by the Rev. William Crawford. (M.R.)

Henderson, Robert, bachelor, and Frankey Savage, spinster, June 12, 1779. James Henderson, surety. Consent of Frankey.

Henderson, William, and Lucey Fortune, July 17, 1796. Eddy Fortune, surety. Consent of her father, Thomas Fortune. Certificate of marriage by the Rev. William Crawford. (M.R.)

Henderson, William, and Polly Clarke, spinster, June 16, 1800. Robert Henderson, surety.

Hendley, James, bachelor, and Else Dinwiddie, widow, July 18, 1786. John Murrell, surety. Consent of Else, who signed as "Alecey Dunwoody."

Hendren, Robert, and Mary McCue, spinster, October 27, 1798. Charles McCue, surety. Consent of her father, John McCue.

Hendrick, Byrd, bachelor, and Caty Baker, spinster, March 31, 1794. Henry Holloway, surety. Consent of her father, Joseph Baker.

Henson, Murry, and Elizabeth Roberts, spinster, September 11, 1797. Joseph Henson, surety. Joseph Henson made oath that his brother, Murry Henson, was 21 years of age. Consent of her father, John Roberts.

Higginbotham, Aaron, and Nancy Croxton, spinster, December 4, 1775. Aaron Higginbotham, Caleb Higginbotham and Gabriel Penn, sureties.

Higginbotham, Benjamin, bachelor, and Mary Gatewood, spinster, January 21, 1782. Larkin Gatewood, surety.

Higginbotham, Francis, bachelor, and Dolly Gatewood, daughter of Larkin Gatewood, December 1, 1783. Samuel Higginbotham, surety. Consent of his father, Benjamin Higginbotham. Certificate of marriage by the Rev. Benjamin Coleman, December 2, 1783. (Order Book 1782-1784, p. 210.)

Higginbotham, James, bachelor, and Rachel Campbell, spinster, May 30, 1779. James Higginbotham and John Loving, Jr., sureties. Consent of her mother, Charity Campbell.

Higginbotham, John, and Rachel Banks, July 9, 1767. William Horsley, surety. Consent of her father, Gerrard Banks.

Higginbotham, John [Satterwhite], (son of Samuel), and Ann Stanton Higginbotham, spinster, December 17, 1792. John Higginbotham, surety. Consent of her father, John Higginbotham. Certificate of marriage by the Rev. William Crawford. (M.R.)

Higginbotham, Joseph, and Rachel Higginbotham, married by the Rev. Benjamin Coleman, April 16, 1783. (Order Book 1782-1784, p. 111.)

Higginbotham, Joseph, bachelor, and Frances Higginbotham, spinster, December 17, 1788. Benjamin Higginbotham, surety. Consent of her father, Moses Higginbotham, who states that Joseph Higginbotham is a son of Benjamin Higginbotham.

Higgins, Patrick, and Margaret Tennison, March 20, 1792. Thomas Hays, surety. Certificate of marriage by the Rev. Mr. Day, March 21, 1792. (M.R.)

Hill, Dabney, and Elizabeth Tucker, spinster, August 26, 1800. Howard Cash, surety. Consent of Charles and Mary Tucker.

Hill, Ezekiel, bachelor, and Nancy Wills, spinster, January 18, 1790. William Teas, surety. Consent of her father, James Wills.

Hill, John, Jr., bachelor, and Genny Watts, spinster, November 30, 1793. William Watts, surety. Consent of her father, Charles Watts.

Hill, Madison, bachelor, and Polly Day, spinster, August 14, 1790. Samuel Day, surety. Consent of her mother, Mary Ann Day. Consent of Polly.

Hill, Pleasant, and Sally Rippetoe, March 18, 1797. James Hambleton, surety. Murry Hill states that the mother of Sally gave her consent. Peter Rippoto states that the parents of both Pleasant Hill and Sally Rippetoe gave their consent. Certificate of marriage by the Rev. Ro: Jones. (M.R.)

Hill, Samuel, bachelor, and Lucy Mitchell, spinster, January 5, 1786. John Mitchell, surety. Consent of her father, Archibald Mitchell.

Hill, Taliaferro, and Nancy Woodroof, December 20, 1797. William Watson, surety. Consent of her father, David Woodroof. Certificate of marriage by the Rev. Charles Crawford. (M.R.)

Hix, Joseph, bachelor, and Lucretia Childress, spinster, November 3, 1792. Achilles Ballinger, surety. Consent of Lucretia. Certificate of marriage by the Rev. Mr. Woods, November 5, 1792. (M.R.)

Hogg, John, and Susannah ———————, April 14, 1779, in Amherst County, by the Rev. Mr. Crawford. See Susannah Hogg's application for a pension, March 3, 1849, aged 88 years. No M.L.B. of record in Amherst Court.

Hogg, Randol, and Molly Goodrich, December 27, 1797. William Peter, surety. Consent of her father, John Goodrich. Certificate of marriage by the Rev. Charles Crawford, who calls him "Randolph Hogg." (M.R.)

Holeman, Tandy, bachelor, and Elizabeth Abney, spinster, September 30, 1786. William Abney, surety. Consent of her grandfather, Paul Abney. Consent of Elizabeth.

Holladay, Fielding, bachelor, and Mary Clements, spinster, April 22, 1791. William Clements, Jr., surety. Consent of his father, John *Holaday,* for him to marry Mary Clements, daughter of William Clements, Jr.

Hollingsworth, Joseph, bachelor, and Molly Mathews, spinster, March 10, 1789. James Hansbrough, surety. Consent of her father, James Mathews.

Holloway, Robert, and Sarah Penn, spinster, November 18, 1797. George Dillard, surety. Certificate of marriage by the Rev. Charles Crawford. (M.R.)

Horsley, Robert, and Miss Judith Scott, spinster, August 21, 1771. James Wills, surety.

Hosling, Benjamin, bachelor, and Mary Gatewood, spinster, November 10, 1783. William Pollard, surety. Consent of her father, Richard Gatewood.

Hotchkiss, Gerard, bachelor, and Betsey Knight, spinster, June 6, 1791. William Knight, surety.

Houchen, Jesse, bachelor, and Mary Ann Goode, spinster, December 21, 1793. Alexander Gillaspie, surety. Consent of her mother, Feby Goode. Certificate of marriage by the Rev. Ezekiel Campbell, who calls him "Jesse *Houchens."*

Howard, Claiborn, bachelor, and Sally Martin, spinster, April 26, 1790. George Wooddy, surety. Consent of her father, James Martin.

Howard, Peter, widower, of Rockbridge County, and Sarah Strickland, spinster, October 29, 1791. Joseph Strickland, surety.

Howard, William, bachelor, and Amy Powell, widow, December 4, 1783. Peter Carter, surety. Consent of Amy. Certificate of marriage by the Rev. Benjamin Coleman, December 6, 1783. (Order Book 1782-1784, p. 210.)

Hudson, George, and Nancy Bowles, spinster, February 8, 1800. Charles Bowles, surety. Rush Hudson made oath that George Hudson was over 21 years of age.

Hudson, Joshua, widower, and Bethany Cash, spinster, November 30, 1789. Hany Camden, surety. Consent of Bethany. Consent of Richard Oglesby.

Hudson, Joshua, Jr., and Elizabeth Banks, November 1, 1784. Joshua Hudson, surety. Certificate of marriage by the Rev. Benjamin Coleman, November 5, 1784. (Order Book 1784-1787, p. 60.)

Hudson, Robert, and Lucy Galaspie, spinster, daughter of George Galaspie, October 25, 1779. Sherred Moore Galaspie, surety. Consent of her father, George Galaspie.

Huffman, John, and Milley Ship, August 24, 1780. George Blain, surety. Consent of Milley.

Hughs, Harrison, and Nancey Tinsley, spinster, October 6, 1798. Isaac Tinsley, surety. Consent of her father, William Tinsley.

Hunter, David, and Margaret Cameron, married by the Rev. Benjamin Coleman, January 8, 1784. (Order Book 1782-1784, p. 210.)

Hunter, Robert, bachelor, of Campbell County, and Nancy Ellis, spinster, October 1, 1793. Charles Ellis, Jr., surety. Consent of her father, Josiah Ellis. Certificate of marriage by the Rev. Mr. Crawford. (M.R.)

Hurt, Garland, bachelor, and Betsey Ann Tucker, spinster, February 4, 1788. John Watson, surety. Consent of John Hurt. Consent of her father, Matthew Tucker.

Innis, John, and Rachel Campbell, spinster, September 6, 1797. Ambrose Campbell, surety. Certificate of marriage by the Rev. William Crawford. (M.R.)

Irvin, John, and Mary Ann Tucker, spinster, August 14, 1772. Joseph Tucker, surety. Consent of her father, Matthew Tucker.

Irvine, Christopher, and Louise Tucker, September 6, 1778. Joseph Tucker, surety. Consent of her father, Matthew Tucker.

Irvine, Samuel, bachelor, and Ann Fitzhugh Rose, spinster, September 28, 1794. Robert H. Rose, surety. Consent of her father, Hugh Rose.

Irvine, Walter, and Anne Fitzhugh Rose, spinster, September 22, 1790. John N. Rose, surety. Consent of her father, Patrick Rose, dated September 22, 1793.

Jackson, Burwell, and Alley Evans, spinster, September 18, 1799. John Loving and Moses Rucker, sureties. Consent of Alley. James Loving stated that Alley Evans was 30 years of age.

Jacobs, John, bachelor, and Lucy Hill, spinster, March 21, 1796. Nathaniel Hill, surety. Certificate of marriage by the Rev. William Crawford. (M.R.)

Jacobs, John, and Sarah Crawford, spinster, May 21, 1765. Nathaniel Barnet, surety. Consent of her father, David Crawford.

Jacobs, William, bachelor, and Nancy Fitz Gerrall, spinster, November 6, 1795. Bartlett Fitz Gerrald (he signed as *Gerrald*), surety. Consent of Nancy.

Jacobs, William, bachelor, and Margaret McDaniel, spinster, April 22, 1791. John Clarkson, surety. Consent of her father, Daniel McDaniel.

Jarvis, Thomas, bachelor, and Mary Vickers, spinster, August 5, 1789. Bartholomew Staton, surety. Consent of Mary who states she is 24 years of age. Bartholomew Vickers stated that Mary was above 21 years of age.

Jennings, Robert, and Sophia Rucker, December 23, 1797. Isaac Rucker, Jr., surety. Consent of her father, Ambrose Rucker.

Johns, John, bachelor, and Oney Dillard, spinster, June 18, 1790. Nathaniel Guttry, surety. Consent of her father, William Dillard.

Johns, Robert, bachelor, and Elizabeth Lyon, spinster, daughter of Elisha Lyon, April 6, 1779. William Booth, surety. Consent of her father, Lishalion (*Elisha Lyon.*)

Johns, Thomas, bachelor, and Mary Mehone, spinster, April 6, 1779. William Booth, surety. Consent of her father, Daniel Mehone.

Johnson, Benjamin, bachelor, and Molly Bowles, spinster, August 2, 1784. Isaac Rucker, surety. Consent of her father, Knight Bowles.

Johnson, Benjamin, and Ann Wright, spinster, October 3, 1799. George Wright, surety. Consent of her parents, Achilles and Nancy Wright. Certificate of marriage by the Rev. James Boyd. (M.R.)

Johnson, Isham, and Sally Pamplin, spinster, November 13, 1800. James Evans, surety. Consent of Sally who stated she was 22 years of age. Certificate of marriage by the Rev. James Boyd. (M.R.)

Johnson, John, bachelor, and Mary D. Bell, widow, June 8, 1793. Walter Christian, surety. Consent of Mary D. Certificate of marriage by the Rev. William Dameron, June 13, 1793. (M.R.)

Johnson, John, bachelor, and Penelope Harper, spinster, June 22, 1789. William Harper, surety. Consent of her mother, Judith Harper.

Johnson, John, and Nancy Brown, March 19, 1792. Nathaniel Powell, surety. Consent of her father, Adam Brown.

Johnson, Peter, bachelor, and Nancy Lively, spinster, April 5, 1784. Joseph Lively, surety.

Johnson, Tandy, bachelor, and Salley Bibb, spinster, August 4, 1784. William Bibb, surety. Certificate of marriage by the Rev. Joseph Ballinger, August 5, 1784. (Order Book 1782-1784, p. 403.)

Johnson, Thomas, of Buckingham County, and Mary Stovall, October 10, 1792. James Christian, surety. Consent of Mary.

Johnson, William, bachelor, and Dicey Wood, spinster, August 22, 1792. John Martin, surety. Consent of Stephen Johnson and William Wood.

Johnson, William, and Elizabeth Bibb, spinster, October 20, 1798. Thomas Bibb, surety. Consent of his father, William Johnson. Consent of her mother, Elizabeth Bibb. Certificate of marriage by the Rev. William Crawford. (M.R.)

Jones, Charles, bachelor, and Elizabeth Galaspie, spinster, December 5, 1785. Chesley Kinney, surety. Consent of her father, George *Gillaspie.*

Jones, John, bachelor, and Elizabeth Wren, spinster, December 25, 1783. Charles Jones, surety. Consent of her father, Nicholas Wren.

Jones, John, and Rachel Campbell, married by the Rev. William Crawford, 1797. (M.R.)

Jones, Lane, bachelor, and Catherine Eubanks, spinster, October 2, 1792. John Ware, surety. Consent of her father, Ambrose *Eubank.* Certificate of marriage by the Rev. Mr. Crawford. (M.R.)

Jones, Nathaniel Teller, bachelor, and Nancey Ray, spinster, November, 17, 1794. William Ray, surety.

Jones, Nicholas, and Ammareller Camblin, married July 26, 1782, by the Rev. Benjamin Coleman. (Order Book 1782-1784, p. 1.) In her application for a pension, April 4, 1838, Ammareller (or Anna R. C.) Jones, states that she was married in Amherst at the house of her father, John Camden, she believes July 3, 1783.

Jones, Richard, bachelor, and Polly McDaniel, spinster, January 1, 1797. John McDaniel, surety.

Jones, William, bachelor, and Elizabeth Mahone, spinster, September 6, 1791. Daniel Mahone, surety.

Jones, William, bachelor, and Nancy Wren, spinster, November 27, 1785. John Jones, surety. Consent of her father, Nicholas Wren.

Joplin, James, bachelor, and Nancy Martin, spinster, October 21, 1793. Benjamin Childress, surety. Consent of her father, Pleasant Martin.

Jopling, James, and Sally Ball, spinster, November 26, 1799. Daniel Farguson, surety. Consent of her father, William Ball. Daniel Farguson made oath that James Jopling was 21 years of age.

Jopling, Ralph and Elizabeth Forguson, natural daughter of Bransford West, December 17, 1798. Bransford West, surety.

Jopling, Thomas, Jr., and Sarah Stevens, spinster, April 6, 1772. Edmund Wilcox, surety.

Jopling, Thomas, Jr., bachelor, and Mary Stevens, spinster, November 22, 1790. James Stevens, Jr., surety. Consent of her father, James Stevens, Sr.

Jordan, William (he signed as "Jordain"), bachelor, and Sarah Watts, spinster, February 4, 1792. James Christian, surety. Consent of her father, Stephen Watts. Certificate of marriage by the Rev. Mr. Crawford. (M.R.)

Joyner, Peter, bachelor, and Milly Dillard, spinster, February 20, 1795. Larkin London, surety, who made oath that Milly was over 21 years of age.

Kelley, Benjamin, bachelor, and Nancy Jarrell, spinster, March 2, 1790. James Kelley, surety. Consent of her father, David Jarrell.

Kelley, James, bachelor, and Elizabeth Sledd, spinster, November 6, 1787. William Sledd, surety. Consent of her father, John Sledd.

Kennedy, Jesse, and Susannah Dillard, spinster, October 17, 1780. Edm. Wilcox, surety. Consent of her father, Joseph Dillard.

Kennerly, Joseph, and Sally Christian, spinster, April 26, 1800. Drury Christian, surety. Consent of her mother, Mary Christian.

Kerr, James, widower, and Susannah Rodes, widow, November 20, 1795. Nathan Crawford, surety. Certificate of marriage by the Rev. William Crawford. (M.R.)

Key, John, and Belinda Milstred, July 15, 1797. John B. Mays, surety. Consent of his father, Martin Key, for him to marry Belinda Milstred, daughter of Elizabeth Milstred. Certificate of marriage by the Rev. Charles Crawford. (M.R.)

Key, Martin, Jr., and ———— (no name), December 17, 1773. Bond is endorsed: "Key to Pollard."

Key, Thomas, and Frances Garrot, spinster, May 4, 1773. Edmund Wilcox, surety.

Key, William Waller, bachelor, and Elizabeth Alford, spinster, December 20, 1790. John Alford, surety. Consent of William Alford.

King, Archibald, and Anner Milstead, June 10, 1797. Joseph Milstead, Jr., surety. Consent of her mother, Elizabeth Milstead.

King, Jesse, and Lucey Abner, December 22, 1800. Major King, surety. Consent of John *Abney* and Patman *Abner.*

King, Major, bachelor, and Seley Pucket, spinster, December 27, 1788. William Burnett, surety. Consent of her father, John Pucket.

King, Zachariah, and Lucresey (Lucretia) Puckett, spinster, January 14, 1800. Jacob King, surety. Consent of her mother, Lucresey (Lucretia) Puckett. Certificate of marriage by the Rev. Wm. Crawford. (M.R.)

Kinney, Chesley, bachelor, and Mary Edmonds, spinster, September 17, 1791. William Loving, surety. Consent of her father, Samuel *Edmunds.*

Knight, Andrew, bachelor, and Jane Tuggle, spinster, January 7, 1783. Henry Tuggle, surety. Consent of her father, John Tuggle.

Knight, Austin, see *Orsson Knight.*

Knight, Orsson (Austin), bachelor, and Betsy Ham, spinster, February 24, 1789. Francis Wood, surety. Consent of her father, Stephen Ham.

Knight, William, bachelor, and Margaret Dawson, spinster, March 8, 1796. William Dawson, surety. Consent of her father, Henry Dawson, Sr. Certificate of marriage by the Rev. William Crawford (M.R.)

Knight, William, bachelor, and Temperance Bibb, spinster, November 9, 1783. John Bibb, surety. Consent of his father, John *Night*. Consent of her mother, Sarah Bibb. Certificate of marriage by the Rev. Charles Clay, November 11, 1783. (Order Book 1782-1784, p. 200.)

Lackey, John, bachelor, and Anne Watson, spinster, October 31, 1791. James Penn, surety. Consent of her father, Edward Watson.

Lain, James, and Catherine Eubank. Certificate of marriage by the Rev. Mr. Crawford, 1792. (M.R.)

Lain, Joseph, and Patsey Wright, September 30, 1795. George Burks, surety. Consent of her father, Philip Wright. Certificate of marriage by the Rev. John Bonner, September 30, 1795. (M.R.)

Lain, William, Jr., bachelor, and Mary Lain, spinster, July 1, 1794. William S. Crawford, surety. Consent of his father, James *Lane,* for him to marry Mary *Lane,* daughter of William *Lane* (Waterman).

Laine, John, bachelor, and Lucy Ballow, widow, March 21, 1789. William Lavender, surety. Consent of Lucy.

Laine, John, and Sarah Lackland, married by the Rev. Benjamin Coleman, December 23, 1782. (Order Book 1782-1784, p. 73.)

Laine, Randolph, bachelor, and Mary Robertson, spinster, September 18, 1789. William Laine, surety. Consent of her father, Arthur *Roboson.*

Laine, Thomas, and Milley Lain, July 7, 1798. William Laine, surety. William Layn made oath that Thomas *Layn,* Jr., was 21 years of age. Certificate of marriage by the Rev. Walter Christian. (M.R.)

Laine, Thomas, Jr., and Mary Stratton, spinster, February 26, 1780. Isaac Stratton, surety. Consent of her father, Henry Stratton.

Laine, William, widower, and Hannah Garven, spinster, May 5, 1788. Stephen Watts, surety.

Laine, William, widower, and Rebeccah Berry, spinster, August 5, 1794. Adamson Berry, surety, who made oath that Rebeccah was of lawful age and had given her consent.

Lancaster, John, Jr., see John Lankester.

Landrum, James, bachelor, and Mary Clark Alford, spinster, December 13, 1787. William Alford, surety.

Landrum, Joseph, bachelor, and Sally Fielden, spinster, January 9, 1796. Joshua Willoughby, surety. Consent of her parents, Francis and Anny Fielden.

Landrum, Thomas, Jr., bachelor, and Dolly Alcock, spinster, November 22, 1780. Richard Alcock, surety.

Lane, Joseph, and Patsey Wright, September 30, 1795, by Rev. Jno. Bonner, (M.R.) See Joseph Lain.

Lane, William, and Judith Gatewood, spinster, January 13, 1800. Joseph Layne, surety. Consent of her mother, Sarah Gatewood.

Langham, John, bachelor, and Leddey Smith, spinster, February 4, 1793. Reuben Thomas Mitchell, surety. Consent of his parents, Benedick and Nelly *Lanhaum*. Consent of her parents, Childers and Fanny Smith.

Lankester, John, Jr., bachelor (signed as *John Lancaster, Jr.*), and Lucy Parrock, spinster, December 4, 1790. David Parrock, surety. Consent of her father, Thomas Parrock.

Lankford, Matthew, bachelor, and Philadelphia Lyon, spinster, December 19, 1796. William Lankford, surety. Consent of her father, Peter Lyon.

Lavender, Charles, Jr., bachelor, and Lucy Ballow, spinster, December 21, 1785. John Taliaferro, surety. Consent of his mother, Milly Lavender. Consent of her father, Thomas Ballow.

Lawhorn, George, and Nancy Parsons, March 18, 1797. William Lawhorn, surety. Certificate of marriage by the Rev. Charles Crawford.

Lawless, Richard, widower, and Elizabeth Goodrich, spinster, June 25, 1785. Peter Carter, surety. Consent of her parents, James and Margaret Goodrich.

Lawless, William, bachelor, and Susannah Carter, spinster, August 25, 1795. James Carter, surety, who made oath that Susannah (his sister) was 21 years of age. Mary Ann Carter certifies that Susannah was born August 24, 1773. Certificate of marriage by the Rev. Charles Crawford. (M.R.)

Lawson, John, and Susannah Stinnett, married by the Rev. Benjamin Coleman, February 7, 1783. (Order Book 1782-1784, p. 102.)

Lea, Ferdinand (he signed as "Ferdinand Leigh"), bachelor, and Elizabeth Cash, spinster, December 19, 1796. Benjamin Rogers, surety. Bartlett Cash made oath that Elizabeth was born January 25, 1770.

Leak, Samuel, and Elizabeth Penn, married by the Rev. Benjamin Coleman, October 16, 1783. (Order Book 1782-1784, p. 201.)

Lee, Francis, bachelor, and Nancy Penn, spinster, November 1, 1786. John Taliaferro, surety. Consent of her father, John Penn.

Lee, George, and Elizabeth Shelton, spinster, January 21, 1772. Richard Shelton and George Penn, sureties.

Lee, James, and Ann Powell, February 20, 1792. Jesse Woodroof, surety. Consent of her father, Richard Powell. Consent of Joseph Dawson and John Wiatt, as to James Lee, minor.

Lee, James, bachelor, of Caswell County, N. C., and Frankey Rucker, spinster, January 25, 1786. Ambrose Rucker, Jr., surety. Consent of her father, Ambrose Rucker, who calls her *Franka* Rucker.

Lee, Richard, bachelor, and Frankey Harrison, spinster, December 4, 1780. William Tucker, surety. Consent of George Lee, as to Richard Lee. Consent of her mother, Frances Harrison, and her guardian, Reuben Harrison.

Lee, William, and Susanna Dawson, September 3, 1770. Cornelius Sale, surety. Consent of her father, Joseph Dawson.

Leflear, Joseph, bachelor, and Mary Mehone, spinster, December 26, 1791. Daniel Mehone, surety.

Lemaster, Abraham, bachelor, and Sarah Wood, spinster, daughter of John Wood, September 26, 1781. Francis Wood, surety. Consent of her father, John Wood.

Lemaster, Eleazer, bachelor, and Machell Tacket, spinster, September 4, 1786. John Lemaster, surety.

Letcher, James, and Milly Key, January 6, 1771. William Willson, surety. Consent of her father, Henry Key.

Lewis, Charles, and Sally Nevil, May 27, 1796. James Nevil, surety. Consent of Sally.

Lilly, Gabriel, bachelor, and Judith Perry, spinster, January 18, 1796. Joseph Wrenn, surety. Consent of her mother, Susanna Perry. Bartlett Eads made oath that Gabriel was 21 years of age. Certificate of marriage by the Rev. William Crawford. (M.R.)

Lilly, Thomas, bachelor, and Rachel Brown, spinster, January 17, 1793. Rice Brown, surety. Consent of her father, James Brown. Certificate of marriage by the Rev. Mr. Campbell. (M.R.)

Litterall, William, bachelor, and Elizabeth Witt, spinster, June 30, 1787. Littleberry Witt, surety. Consent of her parents, John and Elizabeth Witt.

Litterell, John, bachelor, and Anis Jackson, spinster, August 12, 1789. Richard Litterell, surety. Consent of her father, Peter Jackson.

Lively, John, bachelor, and Clara Carnall, spinster, August 19, 1794. Peter Johnson, surety. Consent of her mother, Mary Shaw. Certificate of marriage by the Rev. Ezekiel Campbell.

Lively, Joseph, Jr., and Salley Tiller, spinster, daughter of William Tiller, November 4, 1784. William Tiller, surety.

Lively, Mark, bachelor, and Mary Hill, spinster, November 30, 1791. Joseph Lively, Jr., surety. Consent of her father, John Hill.

Lively, Robert Cash, bachelor, and Elizabeth Bethel, spinster, August 20, 1783. Thomas Lively, surety. Consent of her father, John Bethel.

Lobban, John, and Jean McNight, December 17, 1792. John McCarter, surety. Consent of her father, William McNight.

Lobban, William, bachelor, and Mary Ware, widow, November 23, 1795. James Lobban, surety. Consent of Mary. James Lobban made oath that William was 21 years of age.

Lockard, Butler, bachelor, and Mary Ann Ware, October 26, 1786. Charles Carter, surety. Consent of Mary Ann.

Lockart, William, bachelor, and Susannah Grady, spinster, December 8, 1789. William Teas, surety. Consent of Susannah.

London, Lavender, and Jane Wright, spinster, April 21, 1800. Samuel Edmunds, Jr., surety. John Wright made oath that Jane was over 21 years of age. Certificate of marriage by the Rev. James Boyd. (M.R.)

London, Larkin, bachelor, and Mary Dillard, spinster, January 2, 1790. Notley Maddox, surety. Consent of her father, William Dillard.

Long, William, bachelor, and Elizabeth Callaway, spinster, September 23, 1794. (Name of surety partly eaten out and illegible.) Certificate of marriage by the Rev. Charles Crawford. (M.R.)

Lonogan, James, bachelor, and Elizabeth Stratton, spinster, June 15, 1789. William Bryan, surety. Consent of Henry Stratton.

Lovegrove, William, widower, and Ann Cartwright, spinster, March 23, 1794. Samuel Brown, surety. Consent of Ann.

Loving, George, bachelor, and Mildred Stevens, spinster, October 17, 1785. James Stevens, surety.

Loving, James, and Nancy Loving, spinster, November 18, 1799. Richard C. Pollard, surety. Consent of her father, John Loving. Certificate of marriage by the Rev. William Crawford. (M.R.)

Loving, John, and Rose Taliaferro, December 18, 1797. Roderick Taliaferro, surety. Consent of her father, Charles Taliaferro. Certificate of marriage by the Rev. Charles Crawford. (M.R.)

Loving, Samuel, and Elizabeth Watts, spinster, December 5, 1800. Spotswood Garland, surety. Consent of her father, Stephen Watts.

Loving, William, and Elizabeth Hargrove, spinster, September 21, 1763. Augustine Seaton, surety.

Loving, William, bachelor, and Sarah Taliaferro, seamstress, April 30, 1792. Zachs. Taliaferro, surety. Consent of her father, Charles Taliaferro.

Lunsford, William, Jr., bachelor, and Rachel Mathews Goad, spinster, October 28, 1786. John Taliaferro, surety. Consent of her mother, Hannah Burden. Consent of his father, William *Lunceford,* Sr. Consent of Rachel.

Luster, William, bachelor, and Elizabeth Bailey, spinster, November 30, 1796. Elijah Staton, surety.

Lyle, John, and Florence Reid, spinster (of lawful age), June 4, 1767. Henry Rose, Gent., surety. Consent of Florence. Certificate of Alexander Miller, Henry Rose and John Loving that they believe Florence to be of lawful age.

Lyon, Alexander, of Culpeper County, bachelor, and Judith Hill, spinster, October 7, 1786. Francis Woods, surety. Consent of his

father, William Lyon, of Culpeper County. Consent of her
parents, William and Susannah Hill.
Lyon, Joseph, and Rebecca Bonnel, married by the Rev. Benjamin
Coleman, April 11, 1792. (M.R.)

Mackey, Michael, bachelor, and Peggy Davis, spinster, June 6, 1791.
Nathaniel Parris, surety. Consent of her father, Thomas Davis.
Maddox, John, and Betsey Campbell, spinster, March 17, 1800. Notley
W. Maddox, surety.
Magan, Joseph, bachelor, and Susannah Hall, spinster, December 19,
1795. Moses Hall, surety.
Magann, John, and Milly Goodwin, May 12, 1798. John Mahone,
surety, who made oath that Milly Goodwin, "daughter of George
Goodwin, was 21 years of age."
Males, John, widower, of Rockbridge County, and Alcey Burks, widow,
November 29, 1792. Henry Peyton, surety. Certificate of mar-
riage by the Rev. Mr. Dameron. (M.R.)
Marr, Alexander, bachelor, and Matilda Rucker, spinster, December
27, 1796. Isaac Rucker, surety. Consent of her father, Ambrose
Rucker.
Marr, Alexander, bachelor, and Sally Brockman, spinster, November
27, 1790. John Brockman, surety.
Marr, James, of Orange County, bachelor, and Betty Rucker, spinster,
January 3, 1791. Isaac Rucker, surety. Consent of her father,
Ambrose Rucker.
Marr, Thomas, and Polly Sledd, spinster, February 15, 1799. William
Sledd, surety. Consent of her father, John Sledd.
Martin, Azariah, and Mary Rodes, spinster, March 10, 1772. William
Martin, surety, who made oath that Mary was of lawful age.
Consent of Mary.
Martin, Azariah, Jr., of Madison County, bachelor, and Lucy Rodes,
spinster, April 20, 1791. Azariah Martin, surety. Consent of her
father, Charles Rodes.
Martin, Edward, and Polly Warwick, May 7, 1792. Daniel Warwick,
surety. Consent of her father, Abraham Warwick.
Martin, George, bachelor, and Milley Eads, spinster, December 24,
1788. Andrew Wright, surety. Consent of her father, Abraham
Eads, of Albemarle County. James Wood made oath that Milley
was over 21 years of age.
Martin, George, bachelor, and Sarah Fox, spinster, May 17, 1788.
Samuel Fox, surety. Consent of his father, Sherod Martin. Con-
sent of her father, Samuel Fox.
Martin, George, bachelor, and Barbary Woods, spinster, June 17, 1793.
Consent of Barbary. Certificate of marriage by the Rev. Mr.
Crawford. (M.R.)
Martin, Gideon, widower, and Franky Innis, spinster, March 13, 1789.
John Innis, surety.

Martin, Gideon, bachelor, and Mary Housright, spinster, September 23, 1793. George Martin, surety. Consent of her father, John Housright.

Martin, James, and Rebecca Wills, spinster, February 4, 1799. Lawrence Wills, surety. Consent of her father, James Wills. Certificate of marriage by the Rev. William Crawford. (M.R.)

Martin, James, bachelor, and Polly Giles, spinster, January 5, 1795. William Giles, surety. Certificate of marriage by the Rev. Ezekiel Campbell, *1794*. (M.R.)

Martin, John, bachelor, and Anne Rodes, daughter of Charles Rodes, December 12, 1782. William Martin, surety. Consent of her father, Charles Rodes, Sr.

Martin, John, and Ann Page, spinster, November 22, 1797. Dillard Page, surety, who made oath that his sister, *Anne* was over 21 years of age. Certificate of marriage by the Rev. William Crawford. (M.R.)

Martin, John, bachelor, and Susannah H. Ball, spinster, December 21, 1794. Lewis Ball, surety, who testified that Susannah Huse Ball was upwards of 21 years of age. (Bond is not signed.) Certificate of marriage by the Rev. Ezekiel Campbell. (M.R.)

Martin, Josiah, and Sarah England, October 6, 1795. William Martin, surety, who made oath that Sarah England was 21 years of age. Certificate of marriage by the Rev. Charles Crawford. (M.R.)

Martin, Kiah, and Dicey Stratton, spinster, November 4, 1794. John Stratton, surety.

Martin, Obediah, bachelor, and Ann New, spinster, January 17, 1791. George Martin, surety. Consent of her mother, Sarah New.

Martin, Pleasant, and Rebecca Jopling, spinster, October 2, 1775. James Hill, surety.

Martin, Pleasant, bachelor, and Betsey Innes, spinster, November 23, 1791. John Innes, surety.

Martin, Ralph, and Sigismundi Price, March 1, 1800. James Woods, surety.

Martin, Robert, widower, and Suky Thusler, spinster, September 19, 1789. John Thusler, surety. Consent of her mother, Ellenor Thusler.

Martin, William, bachelor, and Patsey Key Daverson, spinster, December 8, 1789. Charles Rodes, Jr., surety. Consent of Patsey Key.

Massey, John, and Susannah Wright, January 1, 1779, in Amherst. See Thomas Massey's application for a pension, September 24, 1853. No M. L. B. of record in Amherst Court.

Mathews, Joseph, bachelor, and Lidday Kesterson, spinster, October 25, 1787. William Kesterson, surety. Consent of her father, William Kesterson.

Matthews, John, and Dosha Nash, July 17, 1798. Thomas Nash, surety. John Phillips made oath that Dosha was 21 years of age.

Matthews, William, bachelor, and Mary Bibb, spinster, January 24, 1789. William Bibb, surety.

Maxey, John, bachelor, and Lucretia Edee Tucker, daughter of Matthew Tucker, December 28, 1779. Christopher Irvine, surety. Consent of her father, Matthew Tucker.

Mays, Charles, bachelor, and Rhodey Cash, spinster, September 24, 1791. Howard Cash, surety. Consent of her mother, Tabitha Cash, who calls her "Rhoda Cash."

Mays, James, bachelor, and Lucresa Wade, spinster, January 24, 1786. Ballinger Wade, surety. Consent of her guardian, Richard Ballinger, who calls her "Luciesa Wade."

Mays, Jesse, bachelor, and Susannah Wright, spinster, December 20, 1785. John Mays, surety. Consent of Susannah.

Mays, Jesse, and Frances Hill, spinster, December 23, 1800. Dabney Hill, surety. Consent of Elizabeth Hill. Certificate of marriage by the Rev. John Young, Dec. 25, 1800. (M.R.)

Mays, John, bachelor, and Milly Reppeto, spinster, December 30, 1794. James Reppeto, surety. Consent of her parents, Peter and Sary Reppeto. Certificate of marriage by the Rev. Ezekiel Campbell. (M.R.)

Mays, Joseph, bachelor, and Mary Mays, spinster, October 3, 1791. Robert Mays, surety.

Mays, Lewis, and Caty Campbell, spinster, February 17, 1800. Peter Campbell, surety. Certificate of marriage by the Rev. James Boyd. (M.R.)

Mays, Moses, and Lucy Wright, spinster, April 9, 1800. Jesse Mays, surety. Consent of her father, Minis Wright. Certificate of marriage by the Rev. James Boyd. (M.R.)

Mays, Richard, bachelor, and Pattey Evans, spinster, August 10, 1793. William Bolling, surety. Consent of her father, William Evans. Certificate of marriage by the Rev. Mr. Crawford. (M.R.)

Mays, Robert, and Betsey Campbell, spinster, December 16, 1800. Tandy Campbell, surety. Consent of her father, Ambrose Campbell. Certificate of marriage by the Rev. James Boyd. (M.R.)

Mays, Robert, widower, and Susannah Wade, spinster, September 11, 1780. Richard Ballinger, surety. Consent of Susannah.

Mays, William, bachelor, and Janney Swinney, spinster, March 3, 1788. Micajah Swinney, surety. Consent of her mother, Rosannah Swinney, who calls her "Jane."

Mays, William, and Mary Brown, married by the Rev. Joseph Ballinger, May 15, 1783. (Order Book 1782-1784, p. 122.)

Megan, Archibald, and Elizabeth Whittin, December 18, 1797. John Mahone, surety. Consent of her mother, Mary *Whitin*. John Mahone made oath that Archibald Megan was 21 years of age.

Mehone, John, bachelor, and Sally Pendleton, spinster, October 13, 1794. Richard Pendleton, surety. Consent of her father, Richard Pendleton, who testifies she is 21 years of age.

Meloney, John, bachelor, and Nancy Campbell, spinster, July 13, 1787. Lawrence Campbell, surety.

Merchant, Stephen, bachelor, and Catharine Downton, spinster, April 7, 1789. Roderick McCullock, surety. Consent of Catharine. James Thomas deposed that he raised Catharine from a small girl, "and that she is now of age to dispose of herself in marriage as she chooses."

Merewether, Francis T., and Catherine Eliza Davies, May 28, 1793. Waddy Cobb, surety. Consent of her father, Henry L. Davies. Certificate of marriage by the Rev. Mr. Crawford. (M.R.)

Michaux, Jacob, bachelor, and Sally Nevil, spinster, February 4, 1765. James Nevil, surety.

Miles, James, and Peggy Pendleton, November 11, 1796. John Mehone, surety. Consent of Peggy, who signed as "Elizabeth Pendleton."

Miller, Alexander, and Martha Reid, spinster, April 24, 1766. Alexander Reid, surety. Consent of Martha.

Miller, Samuel, bachelor, and Sarah Morral, spinster, March 1, 1763. Samuel Morral, Jr., surety. Consent of her father, Samuel Morral, Sr., who states that she is of full age.

Miller, Simon, and Catey Lunsford, Mar. 19, 1792. Nathaniel Powell, surety. Consent of her father, William Lunsford.

Milsted, Zeale, bachelor, and Catherine McCabe, spinster, August 9, 1780. Hugh McCabe, surety. Consent of her mother, Sarah McCabe.

Mills, Jesse, and Lucy Tilman, spinster, August 6, 1765. John Fraser, surety. Consent of her father, Thomas Tilman.

Mills, Jesse, bachelor, and Rachel Hudson, spinster, May 21, 1793. Reuben Hudson, surety. Consent of her father, Joshua Hudson. Certificate of marriage by the Rev. Mr. Crawford. (M.R.)

Mitchell, Archelaus, bachelor, and Milley Burks, spinster, November 19, 1784. Charles Burks, surety. Consent of her mother, Elizabeth Burks. Certificate of marriage by the Rev. Benjamin Coleman, November 20, 1784. (Order Book 1784-1787, p. 60.)

Mitchell, Thomas, bachelor, and Eady Trent, spinster, January 2, 1792. Samuel Hill, surety. Consent of his father, Archelaus Mitchell. Consent of her father, Henry Trent.

Mohone, Thomas, bachelor, and Elizabeth Johnson, spinster, February 16, 1795. William Meuse, surety.

Moland, Jesse, bachelor, and Matilda Bain, spinster, December 25, 1793. Charles Christian, surety. Consent of her father, Johnson Bain.

Montgomery, James, bachelor, and Rachel Shields, spinster, [daughter of John and Margaret (Finley) Shields], September 13, 1791. William Loving, Jr., surety. Consent of her father, John Shields.

Montgomery, John, bachelor, and Mary Morrison, spinster, August 23, 1790. Samuel Lackey, surety. Consent of her father, John Morrison.

Montgomery, John Scott, bachelor, and Jenny Wright, December 29, 1794. John Merry Griffin, surety. Consent of her father, Robert Wright.

Montgomery, Joseph, bachelor, and Elizabeth Harris, spinster, June 3, 1780. Andrew Wright, surety. Consent of her father, Lee Harris.

Montgomery, Matthew, bachelor, and Alice Simson, spinster, March 7, 1769. Robert Montgomery, surety. Consent of her father, William Simson.

Montgomery, Thomas, bachelor, and Fanny Pollard, spinster, July 23, 1787. John Taliaferro, surety. Consent of Fanny. Elizabeth Croucher (her sister) testified that she was 21 years of age.

Moon, John, bachelor, and Betsey Pagett, spinster, October 3, 1791. Richard Fulcher, surety. Consent of Abner Padget. Consent of Betsey, who spelled her name *Padget*.

Moon, Mordecai, bachelor, and Caty Fulcher, spinster, February 9, 1790. Richard Fulcher, surety. Consent of her father, John Fulcher.

Moon, William, bachelor, and Charlott Diggs, spinster, November 3, 1793. William H. Diggs, surety. Consent of her father, John Diggs. Certificate of marriage by the Rev. Mr. Crawford. (M.R.)

Moore, Daniel, bachelor, and Rachel Stone, spinster. December 15, 1786. Samuel Perkins, surety. Consent of her father, Lijah (Elijah) Stone.

Moore, Jesse, bachelor, of Burke County, North Carolina, and Elizabeth Stone, October 30, 1788. Daniel Moore, surety. Consent of his father, Jesse Moore. Consent of her father, Elijah Stone.

Moore, John, and Patience Blankenship, married by the Rev. Mr. Day, February 25, 1792. (M.R.) No M.L.B. of record.

Moore, John, and Agnes Langford, November 8, 1800. Pleasant Langford, surety, who made oath that Agnes was over 21 years of age.

Moore, Joseph, bachelor, and Rebecca Barnett, January 15, 1782. James Barnett, surety. Consent of her father, Robert Barnett.

Moore, Philip, bachelor, and Mary Martin, spinster, June 11, 1788. William Teas, surety. Consent of her father, Benjamin Martin.

Moore, Tandy, bachelor, and Sally Bridgwater, spinster, February 15, 1796. William Moore, surety. Consent of her father, Jonathan Bridgwater. William Moore made oath that Sally was over 21 years of age. Certificate of marriage by the Rev. William Crawford, who calls her "Polly Bridgwater." (M.R.)

Moore, Thomas, bachelor, of Albemarle County, and Sally Powell, widow, October 4, 1790. Richard Perkins, surety. Consent of Sally.

Moore, William, bachelor, and Betsey Bridgwater, spinster, February 3, 1789. Jonathan Bridgwater, surety.

Moorman, Henry, bachelor, of Campbell County, and Elizabeth Upshaw, August 14, 1788. James Christian, surety. Consent of her mother, Elizabeth Upshaw.

Moran, Elijah, bachelor, and Mary Mitchell, spinster, August 3, 1793. Thomas Mitchell, surety. Consent of his father, Nicholas Moran. Consent of her mother, Ann Mitchell.

Moran, Nicholas, Jr., and Sally Cartwright, spinster, December 9, 1799. Ambrose Moran, surety. Consent of her father, John Cartwright. Elijah Moran made oath that Nicholas, Jr., was above 21 years of age.

Morris, Allison, and Nancy Peters, February 4, 1797. John Peters, surety. Consent of her father, William Peters.

Morris, George, bachelor, and Nancy Daniel Wade, spinster, March 16, 1790. John Farrar, surety. Consent of his father, John Morris. Consent of Nancy D. Waid.

Morris, William, bachelor, of Bedford County, and Christian Simmons, spinster, April 30, 1793. John Simmons, surety. Consent of James Simons. Certificate of marriage by the Rev. William Dameron, May 2, 1793. (M.R.)

Morrison, James, bachelor, and Elizabeth Thompson, spinster, December 14, 1790. James Montgomery, surety. Certificate of Nathan Crawford that Elizabeth was a relation of his wife; that she was raised by her grandmother, Mrs. Anderson, since she was six weeks old, when her mother died; "she is now 24 years old." Dated, December 13, 1790.

Morrison, John, bachelor, and Winnifred Morris, spinster, August 24, 1784. John Morris, surety.

Morrison, Joseph H., widower, and Mary Walker, widow, October 7, 1796. James Higginbotham, surety. Certificate of marriage by the Rev. William Crawford. (M.R.)

Morrison, Thomas, bachelor, and Margaret Cox, widow, June 2, 1783. James Woods, surety. Consent of Margaret.

Morrison, William, bachelor, and Mary Perry Morris, spinster, December 27, 1781. John Morris, surety.

Morton, John, bachelor, and Nelly Rucker, spinster, February 6, 1786. John Rucker, surety, who made oath that Nelly was 21 years of age. Consent of Nelly, who stated she was "full 21 years of age."

Moss, Anderson, bachelor, and Lucy Penn, spinster, December 31, 1796. Thomas Penn, surety.

Moss, William, bachelor, and Charlotte Cooper, spinster, February 2, 1789. Nathaniel Powell, surety.

Murray, William, bachelor, of Buckingham County, and Lucy Nevil, spinster, December 31, 1792. Consent of her brother and guardian, James Nevil. Certificate of marriage by the Rev. William Crawford. (M.R.)

Murrell, Jesse, and Sarah Lobban, spinster, February 19, 1798. William Lobban, surety. Consent of her father, John Lobban, Sr.

William Lobban made oath that Jesse Murrell was of lawful age. Certificate of marriage by the Rev. William Crawford.

Murrell, John, Jr., bachelor, and Hannah Mitchell, widow, January 27, 1794. Consent of Hannah who signed as "Hanna Mitchel, widow." Certificate of marriage by the Rev. Ezekiel Campbell, who calls her "*Nancy* Mitchell."

Murrell, John, widower, and Sarah Cuff, widow, February 12, 1791. William Murrah, surety. Consent of Sarah.

Muse, William, widower, and Mary Ann Cox, widow, July 24, 1799. Isham Royalty, surety. Consent of Mary Ann.

McAlexander, John, bachelor, and Agness Burnett, spinster, March 25, 1780. Samuel McAlexander, surety. Consent of her parents, John and Elizabeth Burnett.

McAnally, David, and Nancy Kyle, March 18, 1790, in Amherst, by the Rev. Benj. Berger. See David McAnally's pension application.

McAnally, Elijah, bachelor, and Caty Skelton, spinster, April 12, 1790. John McAnally, surety. Consent of her mother, Ann Skelton. Consent of Caty.

McBride, John, and Elizabeth M. Gilbert, October 28, 1796. Ezekiel Gilbert, surety, who made oath that Elizabeth M. was 21 years of age.

McCabe, Hugh, bachelor, and Elizabeth Burks, widow, January 2, 1786. William Galaspie, surety. Consent of Hugh McCabe and Elizabeth Burks.

McCabe, James, bachelor, and Frances Johns, spinster, October 14, 1794. James Callaway, surety. Consent of Frances. Ambrose Rucker testifies that Frances Johns, "daughter of Robert and Mary Johns," was over 21 years of age.

McCabe, John, bachelor, and Polly Thurmond, spinster, March 5, 1794. Isaac Wright, surety. Consent of her father, Philip Thurmond.

McCarter, John, and Patience Henderson, spinster, February 19, 1798. Samuel Bridgwater, surety. Consent of her father, William Henderson. Certificate of marriage by the Rev. Charles Crawford. (M.R.)

McClancey, James, bachelor, and Ann Staton, spinster, August 19, 1793. Thomas Anderson, surety. Consent of her mother, Lucey Staton. Consent of Ann.

McClure, Alexander, and Nancy (Shepherd) Foster, July 15, 1799. In Amherst? She was the widow of James Foster, a Revolutionary soldier. See pension application of James Foster. No M.L.B. of record in Amherst.

McCullock, Roderick, and Elizabeth Horsley, spinster, May 14, 1768. William Horsley, surety. W. Cabell, Jr., and Joseph Cabell state that they approve of the marriage.

McDaniel, George, bachelor, and Susannah Haynes, spinster, September 6, 1790. Benjamin Taliaferro, surety. Consent of her father, William Haynes.

McGinnis, Hiram, bachelor, and Judith Campbell, February 24, 1795. Thomas P. Thornton, surety.

McLaine, James, bachelor, and Sally Bailey, spinster, December 3, 1787. John Taliaferro, surety. Consent of her father, Philip Bailey for her to marry James *McClain*.

McMahon, John, bachelor, and Rossemon Mary Brabban, widow, September 4, 1786. Moses Wray, surety. Consent of Rossemon.

McNeely, Michael, and Rebeckah Morrison, widow, April 8, 1771. William Patton, surety. Consent of Rebeckah. William Patton made oath that Rebeckah was of lawful age and that she signed the above instrument.

McNeely, William, and Rebecca Barnett, spinster, April 30, 1767. James Barnett, surety. Consent of her father, James Barnett.

McQueen, Luis, bachelor, and Molly Innis, spinster, December 7, 1785. George Purvis, Jr., surety. Consent of her father, John Innis.

Nally, Bennett, bachelor, and Mary Appleburry, spinster, January 26, 1791. William Burford, surety. Consent of Mary, who signed as Mary *Appleberry*. William Burford testified Mary was 21 years of age.

Nash, Abner, of Prince Edward County, and Matilda Penn, July 11, 1792. Thomas Haskins, surety. Consent of her father, Gabriel Penn. Certificate of marriage by the Rev. Mr. Crawford. (M.R.)

Netherland, Richard, of Powhatan County, bachelor, and Margaret Woods, spinster, September 24, 1792. Consent of Margaret.

Nevil, Thomas, bachelor, and Elizabeth Tiller, spinster, June 21, 1788. David McGomery, surety. Consent of Elizabeth.

New, Jacob, and Edy Swinney, married by the Rev. Joseph Ballinger, March 17, 1785. Returned at a court held May 2, 1785. (Order Book 1784-1787, p. 111.)

New, James, bachelor, and Martha Tuley, spinster, April 21, 1788. Archelaus Gilliam, surety. Consent of her father, John Tuley.

New, John, bachelor, and Elizabeth Martin, spinster, February 1, 1794. Josiah Haynes, surety. Consent of Elizabeth. Achilles Ballinger and James New testified that Elizabeth was of lawful age.

Newman, Joseph, and Frankey Padget, September 9, 1797. Abner Padget, surety, who made oath that Frankey (his sister) was 21 years of age.

Newman, Joseph, bachelor, and Clary Grady, spinster, November 10, 1784. ——— Cashwell, surety. (First name illegible.) Philip Going and Milley Going, father-in-law and mother of Clary, give their consent, calling Clary "daughter of E d w a r d Grady, deceased."

Nicholas, Lewis, bachelor, of Albemarle County, and Fanny Harris, spinster, April 10, 1793. Joseph Shelton, surety. Consent of William Harris.

Nichols, Robert, and Sally Pryor, May 7, 1795. Nicholas Pryor, surety.

Nichols, Robert, widower, and Fanney Whittin, spinster, March 6, 1797. Jeremiah Whittin, surety.

Nickuls, William, bachelor, and Susannah Shoemaker, spinster, July 6, 1789. Joseph Lively, surety. Consent of her mother, Elizabeth Shoemaker.

Night, George, and Pamelia Evans, spinster, December 30, 1799. Pleasant Evans, surety. Consent of his parents, John and Caty Night.

Nimmo, Robert, bachelor, and Jane Orr, spinster, March 19, 1781. Thomas Watt, surety. Consent of Jane.

Norcutt, Daniel, bachelor, and Rachel Higginbotham, September 13, 1791. Charles Higginbotham, surety. Consent of Rachel, who stated she was the daughter of Moses Higginbotham, deceased. Consent of her mother, Frances Higginbotham.

Norvell, James, and Susannah Hill, spinster, December 18, 1799. James Hill, Jr., surety. Consent of James Hill, Sr. Ezekiel Hill made oath that James Norvell was 21 years of age.

Norvell, William, bachelor, and Ann Wiatt, spinster, July 12, 1794. Robert Holloway, surety. Consent of her father, John Wiatt.

Norvell, William, bachelor (he signed as "Will Norvell, Jr.), and Nancy Wiatt, spinster, July 13, 1794. David S. Garland, surety. (See above.)

Nowlen, James, bachelor, and Susannah Wright, spinster, January 15, 1793. William Tucker, surety. Consent of her father, Isaac Wright.

Obriant, William, and Phebe Hambleton, married by the Rev. William Crawford, 1797. (M.R.) No M.L.B. of record.

Oglesby, Jesse, bachelor, and Celia Witt, spinster, September 15, 1794. David Witt, surety. Consent of David Witt.

Oglesby, Peter, and Sally Pratt, spinster, June 16, 1800. Zachariah Fortune, surety. Consent of her father, Thomas Pratt.

Oglesby, Richard, widower, and ———— Cash, widow, July 6, 1778. Richard Ballinger, surety.

Padgett, Richard, bachelor, and Betsy Moon, spinster, September 11, 1794. Thomas Edwards, surety. Consent of her father, William Moon.

Padgett, William, and Milley Mahon, December 24, 1789. John Padgett, surety. Consent of her father, William *Mehon.*

Page, Dillard, and Polly Clarke, spinster, November 18, 1799. John
Clarke, surety. Certificate of marriage by the Rev. William Crawford. (M.R.)

Page, Francis, bachelor, and Salley Owen, spinster, December 14,
1794. Barnett Owen, surety.

Page, Gabriel, bachelor, and Frances Owen, spinster. No date, but
1794. Barnett Owen, surety. Consent of father, not named. His
or her's? This paper was pinned to the bond of Francis Page,
December 14, 1794. See above.

Page, George (he signed as "George W. Page"), and Henrietta Shepherd, spinster, March 18, 1799. Pleasant Haggard, surety.

Page, Joseph, bachelor, and Lucy F. Corsey, spinster, February 6,
1795. David Clark, surety. Consent of Lucy F. Certificate of
marriage by the Rev. Ezekiel Campbell, who calls her Lucy T.
Cary.

Page, Lindsay, bachelor, and Polley Campbell, spinster, October 31,
1793. Patrick Campbell, surety. Consent of her father, Ambrose
Campbell.

Paget, Beverly, bachelor, and Lucy Fulcher, spinster, July 13, 1791.
Richard Fulcher, surety. Consent of her father, John Fulcher.

Pagett (or Pagitt), Frederick, bachelor, and Lucy Magann, spinster,
April 30, 1787. Joseph Magann, Jr., surety. Consent of John
Magann.

Paggett, Reuben, bachelor, and Catherine Hutcherson, spinster, May
24, 1794. Thomas Edwards, surety. Consent of her father, John
Hutcherson.

Pamplin, James, and Polly Stratton, spinster, October 17, 1799. John
Stratton, surety. Certificate of marriage by the Rev. James Boyd.
(M.R.)

Pamplin, Leroy, and Martha Johnson, spinster, September 7, 1799.
Benjamin Johnson, Jr., surety. Consent of her parents, Benjamin
and Martha Johnson.

Pamplin, William, bachelor, and Mary Wright, spinster, February 19,
1793. James Buck, surety. Consent of Mary.

Parker, Aron, and Jane Veal, spinster, April 8, 1799. Archibald King,
surety. Consent of her parents, William and Elizabeth Veal.

Parker, Henry, and Rebecca Massacra, February 22, 1792. Samuel
Russell, surety. Consent of Mayan Massacra, mother of Rebecca.
Certificate of marriage by the Rev. Mr. Crawford. (M.R.)

Parks, John, bachelor, and Elizabeth Thurmund, spinster. May 17,
1785. John Taliaferro, surety. Consent of her father, Philip
Thurmund. Certificate of marriage by the Rev. B. Coleman,
May 31, 1785. (Order Book 1784--1787, p. 194.)

Parks, William, bachelor, and Milley Burks, spinster, August 1, 1791.
Martin Parks, surety.

Parrish, Samuel, bachelor, and Jean Clarkson, spinster, January 28, 1794. Samuel Hill, surety. Consent of her father, David Clarkson.

Parroch, David, bachelor, and Joice Harper, spinster, October 14, 1785. William Harper, surety. Consent of her mother, Judith Harper.

Parrot, John, bachelor, and Unity Ryan, spinster, June 6, 1792. Charles Ryan, surety, who made oath that Unity was over 21 years of age.

Pasley, Hugh, and Mary Plow, spinster, March 17, 1800. Daniel Cary, surety. Consent of Henry Plow.

Patrick, Thomas F., and E. Witt, married by the Rev. William Crawford, 1799. (M.R.)

Patterson, Alexander, and Mary Campbell, spinster, July 12, 1797. John Cartwright, surety. Consent of *Catron Cammel*. Certificate of marriage by the Rev. William Crawford. (M.R.)

Patterson, David, bachelor, of Bedford County, and Charity Simmons, spinster, April 6, 1793. John Simmons, surety. Consent of James Simmons. Certificate of marriage by the Rev. Mr. Dameron, April 9, 1793. (M.R.)

Paxton, John, and Rebecca Henderson, December 22, 1795. John McCarter, surety. Consent of her father, Robert Henderson.

Payne, Benjamin, widower, and Molley Martin, spinster, April 9, 1789. John Taliaferro, surety. Consent of Molley, who states she is of lawful age.

Payton, Henry, and Elizabeth Pain, married by the Rev. Benjamin Coleman, January 2, 1783. (Order Book 1782-1784, p. 73.)

Payton, James, bachelor, and Elizabeth Cox, spinster, October 6, 1788. Turner Christian, surety. Consent of Elizabeth. Sherred Moore Galaspie and Anthony Street stated that Elizabeth was 21 years of age.

Payton, William, and Nancey Howard, married by the Rev. Benjamin Coleman, November 28, 1782. (Order Book 1782-1784, p. 73.)

Pemberton, John, bachelor, and Elizabeth Witt, widow, July 14, 1787. Andrew Wright, surety. Consent of Elizabeth.

Pendleton, Isaac, bachelor, and Nancy Hardwick, February 16, 1795. Samuel Coleman, surety.

Pendleton, John, bachelor, and Salley Banks, spinster, January 24, 1786. Ballenger Wade, surety. Consent of her father, Linn Banks.

Pendleton, Micajah, and Polly C. Horseley, spinster, December 16, 1799. Robert Wingfield, surety. Consent of Martha Horseley. Micajah Pendleton made oath that he was 21 years of age.

Pendleton, William, bachelor, and Pattsey Cox, spinster, June 7, 1794. Daniel Norcut, surety. Consent of her guardian, Maryan Cox, who calls Pattsey "daughter of Archer Cox, deceased." Certificate of marriage by the Rev. William Dameron, June 8, 1794. (M.R.)

Penn, Abraham, and Ruth Stovall, spinster, March 3, 1767. Daniel Gaines, gentleman, surety.

Penn, George, and Mary Walden, May 25, 1783. Philip Penn, surety. Certificate of marriage by the Rev. Charles Clay, May 29, 1783, who calls them "George Penn, widower," and "Mary Walden, widow, both of Amherst County." (Order Book 1782-1784, p. 136.)

Penn, James, and Nancy Redcross, spinster, August 27, 1799. Rawleigh Penn, surety. Consent of her father, John Redcross.

Penn, James, bachelor, and Mary Major, spinster, December 5, 1791. John Lackey, surety. Consent of Mary.

Penn, Joseph, and Fanny Burras, daughter of Charles Burras. December 4, 1780. John Wright, surety. Consent of her father, Charles Burras.

Penn, Thomas, and Behethland Stevens, September 27, 1796. James Stephens, Jr., surety. Consent of her father, James Stevens, Sr. Certificate of marriage by the Rev. William Crawford. (M.R.)

Penn, Wilson, bachelor, and Frances Taliaferro, spinster, September 8, 1796. Wiatt Smith, surety. Zach. Taliaferro, father of Frances, made oath that she was born in the year 1774. Certificate of marriage by the Rev. William Dameron, September 12, 1796. (M.R.)

Peris and Murphy, married by the Rev. William Crawford, 1795 or 1796. (M.R.)

Perkins, Harding, bachelor, of Buckingham County, and Milly Moore, spinster, November 23, 1790. Benjamin Moore, Jr., surety. Consent of her father, Benjamin Moore.

Perkins, Richard, Jr., bachelor, and Betsey Moore, spinster, daughter of Benjamin Moore, November 12, 1779. George Purvis, surety. Consent of her father, Ben. *Moor.*

Perkins, Samuel, bachelor, and Fanney Stone, November 2, 1784. Richard Perkins, surety. Consent of his father, Richard Perkins. Consent of her father, Elijah Stone.

Perry, William, of Fluvanna County, and Elizabeth Hughes, spinster, January 22, 1799. James Hughes, surety. Consent of her father, Moses Hughes. Certificate of marriage by the Rev. William Crawford. (M.R.)

Peter, John, and Catherine Lane, spinster, January 4, 1800. Allison Morris, surety. Consent of her father, Henry Lane, Sr., and of her mother (not named). Consent of his father, William Peter, who states he is of age.

Peters, Elisha, bachelor, and Jane Tiller, spinster, June 1, 1792. Charles Watts, surety. Consent of her father, William Tiller.

Peters, James, bachelor, and Elizabeth Stevens, spinster, March 11, 1793. Barnett Stevens, surety. Consent of Barnett Stevens.

Peters, Zacharias, bachelor, and Kesiah Lively, spinster, November 18, 1794. Austin Woody, surety. Certificate of marriage by the Rev. Ezekiel Campbell. (M.R.)

Pettus, Thomas, and Rhoda Dawson, July 17, 1792. Pleasant Dawson, surety. Consent of her father, Joseph Dawson.

Peyton, Daniel, and Mary Roach, August 24, 1785. William Gillespie, surety. Consent of his father, Philip Peyton, who states Daniel is of age. Consent of her father, Ashcraft Roach. This is a consent only.

Peyton (or Payton), Daniel, and Nancy Roch (Roach), spinster, August 4, 1784. Philip Thurmond, surety. Consent of his father, Philip Payton. Consent of her father, Ashcraft Roach.

Phelps, Richard, bachelor, and Ann Bell, spinster, February 2, 1789. George Phillips, surety. Consent of his father, William Phelps. Consent of Ann.

Philere, John (he signed as John Felix, which see), and Sally Haynes, ———— 4, 1793. Jesse Haynes, surety. Consent of her father, William Haynes.

Phillips, George, bachelor, and Mary Bell, spinster, daughter of Henry Bell, May 19, 1779. Henry Bell, surety.

Phillips, George, bachelor, and Susanna Campbell, spinster, March 23, 1793. Thomas Brady, surety. Consent of Francis Campbell.

Phillips, George, bachelor, and Margaret Johnston, spinster, January 27, 1795. William Johnston, surety. Consent of her father, Stephen Johnson. Certificate of marriage by the Rev. Ezekiel Campbell. (M.R.)

Phillips, Isaac, and Lucy Goodrich, July 26, 1796. Samuel Goodrich, surety. Consent of her father, James Goodrich.

Phillips, Joel, bachelor, and Caty Poe, spinster, November 27, 1785. Virgil Poe, surety. Consent of her mother, Elizabeth Poe.

Phillips, John, bachelor, and Elpee Evans, January 20, 1790. Samuel Arrington, surety. Consent of her mother, Elizabeth Evans.

Phillips, John, and Rhody Morris, December 19, 1797. Beverley Williamson, surety. Consent of her mother, Anne Phillips. Certificate of marriage by the Rev. Leonard Ballow. (M.R.)

Phillips, Johnson, and Nancy Grisby Grady, August 6, 1792. Philip Lockhart, surety. Consent of Philip Going for his wife Mildred's daughter, Nancy Grigsby Grady to marry Johnson Phillips.

Phillips, Joseph, bachelor, and Jenny Griffin, spinster, December 21, 1795. Lindsey Griffin, surety. Consent of her father, John Griffin. Certificate of marriage by the Rev. William Crawford. (M.R.)

Phillips, Leonard, bachelor, and Elisabeth Turner, November 19, 1792. John Turner, surety. Consent of her father, James Turner. Certificate of marriage by the Rev. Mr. Campbell. (M.R.)

Pickett, Richard, bachelor, of Caroline County, and Elizabeth Burrus, spinster, May 11, 1789.. Joseph Burrus, surety. Consent of her father, Charles Burrus.

Plow, Philip, and Jane Pasley, married by the Rev. Benjamin Berger, October 21, 1800. (M.R.)

Plunket, Benjamin, widower, and Frances Ham, spinster, July 16, 1792. Robert Holloway, surety. Consent of [her father] Stephen Ham. Certificate of marriage by the Rev. William Crawford. (M.R.)

Pollard, Robert, bachelor, and Orany Watts, spinster, December 25, 1778. Thomas Griffin, surety. Consent of her parents, Joseph Dillard and wife. Joseph Dillard states that Orany is of age.

Pollux, James. See Pottox, James.

Pope, Leroy, Jr., bachelor, and Judith Sale, spinster, February 19, 1787. John Taliaferro, surety. Consent of her father, Cornelius Sale.

Pottox, James, and Elizabeth Phillips, married by the Rev. Benjamin Berger, 1782. Returned at a court held August 5, 1782. Mr. Berger spells the name "Pollux." (Order Book 1782-1784, p. 1.)

Powell, Benjamin, bachelor, and Jane Cooper, spinster, November 6, 1783. Nathaniel Powell, surety. Consent of his father, Lucas Powell. Consent of her guardian, William Powell. Certificate of marriage by the Rev. Charles Clay, November 10, 1783. (Order Book 1782-1784, p. 201.)

Powell, Francis, bachelor, and Nancey Whitehead, spinster, November 30, 1784. Thomas Powell, surety. Consent of her father, John Whitehead. Certificate of marriage by the Rev. Joseph Ballinger, December 2, 1784. (Order Book 1784-1787, p. 60.)

Powell, Nathaniel, bachelor, and Elizabeth Chamberlain, widow, July 28, 1781. Thomas Hawkins, surety. Consent of Elizabeth.

Powell, Richard, and Elizabeth Muffett, widow, February 1, 1780. Thomas Powell, surety.

Powell, Thomas, minor, and Sarah Thomas, spinster, October 2, 1782. Wiatt Powell, surety. Consent of James Nevil and Joseph Cabell as to Sarah Thomas.

Powers, John, of Frederick County, and Frances Whitehead, spinster, September 24, 1792. Burcher Whitehead, surety. Consent of Frances.

Price, Thomas, and Elizabeth Ellis, spinster, November 4, 1777. Edmund Wilcox, surety. Consent of her father, Solomon Ellis.

Profitt, Augustin, bachelor, and Elizabeth Robertson, spinster, November 22, 1790. Charles Lain, surety. Consent of his father, David Profitt, Sr. Consent of her father, Arthur Robertson.

Profitt, David, Jr., bachelor, and Sarah Robertson, spinster, July 21, 1787. John Proffitt, surety. Consent of his father, David Profitt. Consent of her father, Robert *Robinson.*

Profitt, John, bachelor, and Margaret Welch, spinster, April 29, 1785. David Profitt, surety. Consent of her father, John Welch. Consent of Margaret.

Profitt, John, widower, and Mary Hopper, spinster, November 4, 1788. Jesse Wright, surety. Consent of her mother, Nancey Hopper.

Profitt, Randolph, and Milley Ball, July —, 1795. Peter Hansbrough, surety. Consent of her parents, John and Elizabeth Ball.

Pryor, David, bachelor, and Lucy Brown, spinster, December 20, 1796. Leroy Brown, surety.

Pryor, Jesse, and Polly Nuckles, November 30, 1796. Robert Nuckles, surety. Consent of his father, Nicholas Pryor.

Pryor, John, and Elizabeth Tucker, spinster, January 30, 1798. Philip Thurmond, surety. Consent of her father, Thomas Tucker.

Pryor, Nicholas, and Salley Paxton, married by the Rev. Benjamin Coleman, December 16, 1782. (Order Book 1782-1784, p. 73.)

Pryor, William, and Sarah Tucker, spinster, December 4, 1797. John Roberts, surety. Consent of her father, Thomas Tucker for her to marry *William Pryor, Jr.* Consent of his father, Nicholas Pryor.

Pryor, William, bachelor, and Elizabeth Wright, spinster, October 13, 1788. Bartlett Cash, surety. Consent of her father, Isaac Wright.

Puckett, Jacob, and Elizabeth Campbell, spinster, October 17, 1800. Mager King, surety. Consent of his father, Jacob *Pucket.*

Puckett, Samuel, and Polly Watkins, June 2, 1798. William Barnett, surety. Consent of his mother, Lucy Puckett. Consent of her father, John Watkins. Certificate of marriage by the Rev. William Crawford. (M.R.)

Pugh, Frederick, bachelor, and Betsey Morris, spinster, November 7, 1785. John Taliaferro, surety. Consent of her parents, John Morris and wife.

Pugh, John, bachelor, and Nancy Stratton, spinster, July 27, 1793. William Lavender, surety. Consent of her father, John Stratton.

Pugh, John, bachelor, and Sarah Morris, spinster, November 30, 1789. John Morris, surety.

Pugh, Thomas, bachelor, and Winnefred Morrison, widow, January 2, 1788. Richard Harvie, surety. Consent of John Pugh. Consent of Winnefred who stated she was of lawful age.

Pugh, Young, and Mary Ann Landrum, March 7, 1792. William Landrum, surety. Consent of Young Landrum. Consent of Mary Ann. William Landrum made oath that Mary Ann, daughter of Young Landrum, was over 21 years of age.

Purvis, Charles, bachelor, and Mary Crisp, spinster, August 1, 1795. William Crisp, surety. Consent of her father (not named).

Purvis, George, and Elizabeth Murphy, October 19, 1795. John Loving, Jr., surety. Consent of Elizabeth. James Murphy made oath that Elizabeth was upwards of 21 years of age.

Purvis, William, and Polly Gregory, December 17, 1792. Charles Purvis, surety.

Ray, Luke, bachelor, and Pamelia Cash, spinster, September 18, 1793. Reuben Franklin, surety. Consent of William Sandidge. Certificate of marriage by the Rev. Mr. Crawford. (M.R.)

Read, Edmund, and Paulina Cabell, spinster, daughter of William Cabell, Esqr., of the County of Amherst, September 13, 1782. William Cabell, Jr., surety. Consent of her father, W. Cabell.

Readmond, Joseph, and Nancy Sorrel, spinster, March 17, 1800. Joseph Lovell, surety. Consent of Elijah Sorrel who states that Joseph Readmond and Nancy Sorrel are each 21 years of age.

Ready, William, and Sarah Dinwiddie, spinster, August 26, 1797. John Burnett, surety. Consent of her parents, James and Alesey Handley. Certificate of marriage by the Rev. William Crawford. (M.R.)

Reed, Jacob, bachelor, and Elizabeth Staton, spinster, May 30, 1792. John Ballew, surety. Consent of her father, William Staton. Certificate of marriage by the Rev. Mr. Campbell. (M.R.)

Reid, Alexander, bachelor, of Bedford County, and Jane Shannon, spinster, March 3, 1790. James Reid, surety. Consent of his father, James Reid. Consent of her father, Thomas Shannon.

Reid, Henry, bachelor, and Elizabeth Gregory, spinster, January 3, 1784. John Gregory, surety.

Reid, John, bachelor, and Elizabeth Coleman, spinster, October 11, 1792. Daniel Coleman, surety. Consent of her father, Ben Coleman. Certificate of marriage by the Rev. Mr. Crawford. (M.R.)

Reid, Jones, widower, and Milly Dawson, spinster, September 10, 1792. James Callaway, surety. Consent of her father, Martin Dawson. Certificate of marriage by the Rev. Mr. Crawford. (M.R.)

Reid, Thomas, and Florence Mills, spinster, December 28, 1771. John Reid, surety. Consent of Florence.

Reynolds, Archelaus, and Elizabeth Rucker, spinster, September 9, 1797. Obediah Reynolds, surety, who made oath that Archelaus was over 21 years of age.

Reynolds, James, widower, and Elizabeth Bolling, spinster, September 1, 1798. James Bolling, surety.

Reynolds, John, bachelor, and Abigail Hardwick Wade, spinster, August 24, 1788. Jeremiah Wade, surety. Consent of Abigail Hardwick Wade. Roderick McCullock testified that Abigail Hardwick was 21 years of age. Elizabeth Fowler testified that Abigail Hardwick was 21 years of age about January 16, 1788.

Rice, William, and Mary Pannell, spinster, November 22, 1798. James Brooks, surety. Consent of her father, Luke Pannell.

Rickets, Mathew, bachelor, and Winnefred Landrum, spinster, November 7, 1791. Benjamin Plunkett, surety. Consent of her father,

Benjamin Landrum. Consent of Winnefred. Certificate of marriage by the Rev. Mr. Coleman, November 9, 1791. (M.R.)

Ridgeway, James, bachelor, and Elizabeth Tennison, spinster, November 8, 1791. Henry Tennison, surety, who made oath that Elizabeth Tennison, daughter of John Tennison, decd., was 21 years of age. Certificate of marriage by the Rev. Mr. Coleman, December 9, 1791. (M.R.) Consent of Elizabeth.

Rippeto, James, bachelor, and Nancy Brown, spinster, November 15, 1790. John Brown, surety. Consent of his father, Peter Rippeto. Consent of her father, John Brown.

Rives, Robert, bachelor, and Peggy Cabell, seamstress, January 18, 1790. Hector Cabell, surety. Consent of her father, W. Cabell.

Roach, Ashcraft, widower, and Elizabeth Fowler, spinster, June 25, 1789. John F. P. Lewis, surety. Consent of Elizabeth.

Roach, Henry, bachelor, and Elizabeth Burks, spinster, May 26, 1791. Richard Burks, surety. Consent of her father, David Burks.

Roach, William, bachelor, and Obedience Burks, spinster, October 20, 1793. David Burks, Jr., surety. Consent of her father, David Burks. Certificate of marriage by the Rev. William Dameron, October 20, 1793. (M.R.)

Roberts, Alexander, and Sarah Shepherd, February 20, 1797. Augustin Shepherd, surety. Consent of her mother, Sarah Shepherd. Certificate of marriage by the Rev. Benjamin Berger. (M.R.)

Roberts, Henry, bachelor, and Fanny Harris, spinster, December 16, 1794. Matthew Harris, Jr., surety, who gives consent as to Fanny Harris.

Roberts, Jacob, bachelor, and Patsey Dodd, spinster, January —, 1796. Josias Dodd, surety. Certificate of marriage by the Rev. Mr. Campbell, who calls him "Jacob Robards."

Roberts, Joseph, widower, and Sally Hardy, spinster, March 22, 1787. John Taliaferro, surety. Consent of her mother, Betsy Hardy, and her brother, Robert Hardy. Consent of Sally.

Roberts, Joseph, widower, and Sarah Woods, widow, March 23, 1781. William Barnett, surety. Consent of Sarah.

Roberts, Zachariah, bachelor, and Sarah Nictherland Harris, spinster, October 24, 1789. John Taliaferro, surety.

Robertson, Leroy, and Mary Wright, spinster, January 9, 1799. David Wright, surety, who made oath that Mary was the daughter of Menos Wright and that she was 21 years of age. Certificate of marriage by the Rev. Walter Christian. (M.R.)

Robertson, Matthew, of Albemarle County, and Catherine McCarter, spinster, December 19, 1800. Thomas Robertson, surety. Consent of Catherine.

Robertson, Thomas, bachelor and Mary McCarter, spinster, October 4, 1779. Alexander Reid, surety. Consent of Mary.

Robinson, Harvey, and Elizabeth Logan, spinster, August 28, 1799. Anthony Logan, surety. John Wilcher made oath that Harvey

Robinson was 21 years of age. Certificate of marriage by the
Rev. Walter Christian, August 29, 1799. (M.R.)

Robinson, Robert, and Nancy Hill, spinster, November 22, 1797. James
Hill, surety.

Robinson, Stephen, bachelor, and Judith Guttery, spinster, July 11,
1789. Nathaniel Guttery, surety. Consent of her father, William
Guttry.

Robinson, Thomas, bachelor, and Elizabeth Laine, spinster, March 17,
1789. Charles Laine, surety. Consent of her father, Thomas
Laine.

Rogers, Robert, and Ann Pamplin, spinster, October 6, 1783. William
Horsley, surety.

Rose, Hugh, Esqr., and Caroline Matilda Jordan, spinster, September
28, 1767. Edmund Wilcox and William Horsley, sureties. Consent of her father, Samuel Jordan.

Rowsey, Archelaus, bachelor, and Elizabeth Nowell, spinster, January
12, 1790. John Wood, surety. Consent of James Rowsey. Consent
of John Nolle.

Rowsey, Leonard, bachelor, and Betsey Cammil Goode, spinster, November 5, 1792. Berry Briant, surety. Consent of Leonard. Consent of Benjamin Goode. Consent of Betsey. Certificate of
marriage by the Rev. Mr. Dameron. (M.R.)

Royalty, Isham, and Patsey Muse, October 30, 1797. William Jones,
surety. Consent of William Muse.

Royalty, John, and Sallie Muse, October 21, 1797. Adam Willie,
surety. Consent of her father, William Muse.

Rozel, Nehemiah, widower, and Ann Van Levan, widow, May 24, 1792.
Patrick Higgins, surety.

Rucker, Ambrose, Jr., bachelor, and Elizabeth Lucas, spinster. January
25, 1786. Thomas Lucas, surety. Consent of his father, Ambrose
Rucker.

Rucker, Ambrose, and Betsey Parks, July 29, 1799. Martin Parks,
surety. John Hill, Jr., made oath that Ambrose Rucker and
Betsey Parks were each 21 years of age.

Rucker, Armistead, and Elizabeth Richerson. Certificate of marriage
by the Rev. John Young, December 28, 1800. (M.R.)

Rucker, Isaac, bachelor, and Mary Higginbotham, spinster, January
28, 1793. David Higginbotham, surety. Consent of her father,
John Higginbotham. Ambrose Rucker certifies that Isaac is of
age. Certificate of marriage by the Rev. William Crawford.
(M.R.)

Rucker, Isaac, Jr., bachelor, and Mary A. Christian, spinster, January
12, 1796. Thomas Woodroof, surety. Consent of her father,
Henry Christian.

Rucker, James, bachelor, and Milley Rucker, spinster, September 14,
1792. Isaac Rucker, surety. Consent of her father, John Rucker.

Rucker, John, and Hannah Phillips, spinster, March 3, 1797. Conyers Phillips, surety. Consent of her father, Conyers Phillips.

Rucker, John, bachelor, and Rachel Rucker, spinster, August 12, 1791. Isaac Rucker, surety. Consent of her father, John Rucker.

Rucker, John, Jr., bachelor, and Nancey Shelton, spinster, March 14, 1788. John Rucker, surety. Consent of her father, Richard Shelton.

Rucker, Moses, bachelor, and Elizabeth Parks, widow, December 29, 1786. Benjamin Plunkett, surety. Consent of Ambrose Rucker. Consent of Elizabeth.

Rucker, Reuben, and Betsy Dawson, August 7, 1792. Nelson Dawson, surety. Consent of her father, Martin Dawson. Consent of Isaac Rucker as to Reuben Rucker. Certificate of marriage by the Rev. Mr. Crawford. (M.R.) Consent of Betsy.

Rucker, Richard, bachelor, and Patsey Hudson, spinster, March 22, 1795. Joshua Hudson, surety. Certificate of marriage by the Rev. Lewis Dawson. (M.R.)

Rucker, Richard, and Margaret Marr, July 16, 1798. Alexander Marr, surety, who made oath that Margaret was 21 years of age.

Russell, James, and Mary Gilmer, married by the Rev. Joseph Ballinger, May 15, 1783. (Order Book 1782-1784, p. 122.)

Ryalty, John, bachelor, and Mary Bowman, spinster, June 7, 1790. Ambrose Rucker, Jr., surety. Consent of her father, Drewry Bowman.

Ryan, Joseph, and Patsey Rose, spinster, May 7, 1799. Patrick Rose, surety.

Rye, Joseph, and Lucy T. Cary, married by the Rev. Ezekiel Campbell, 1794. (M.R.)

Sale, Cornelius, and Janey Dawson, October 20, 1768. John Sale, surety. Consent of her father, Joseph Dawson.

Sale, William, and Viney Duncan, spinster, March 31, 1800. Cornelius Sale, surety. Consent of her father, John Duncan. Certificate of marriage by the Rev. James Boyd. (M.R.)

Sandidge, Benjamin, and Elizabeth Childress, married by the Rev. Benjamin Coleman, October 28, 1783. (Order Book 1782-1784, p. 201.)

Sandidge, William, and Tamsey Cash, married by the Rev. Benjamin Coleman, August 19, 1783. (Order Book 1782-1784, p. 173.)

Saunders, John Merry, bachelor, and Mildred Thompson, widow, April 7, 1790. James Stevens, surety. Consent of Mildred.

Savage, James, bachelor, and Mary Phillips, spinster, December 25, 1787. William Phillips, surety. Consent of her father, John Phillips.

Savage, John, Jr., and Elizabeth Stratton, spinster, September 17, 1800. Notley Smoot, surety, who made oath that John Savage, Jr.,

and Elizabeth Stratton were each over 21 years of age. Certificate
of marriage by the Rev. James Boyd. (M.R.)

Savage, John, and Ann Penn, spinster, October —, 1775. William
Megginson and Edmund Wilcox, sureties.

Scott, Alexander, bachelor, and Ann Williams, spinster, October 7,
1795. William Clark, surety. James Warren made oath that Ann
was 21 years of age.

Scott, Isaac, bachelor, and Elizabeth Miles, spinster, January 21, 1793.
Thomas Stewart, surety. Consent of her father, Joseph Miles.
Certificate of marriage by the Rev. Mr. Crawford. (M.R.)

Scott, Jacob, bachelor, and Milley Franklin, spinster, August 6, 1787.
Samuel Franklin, surety, who made oath that Milley Franklin
"is above the age of 18 years and to the best of his knowledge
exceeds 21 years." Consent of Milley.

Scott, John, and Elizabeth Dillard, spinster, February 10, 1772. James
Dillard, surety.

Scott, John, Jr., of Albemarle County, bachelor, and Elizabeth Rose,
spinster, May 16, 1795. Consent of her father, Charles Rose.
Certificate of marriage by the Rev. Charles Crawford. (M.R.)

Sea (Seay?), Joseph, and Nancy Harvey, married by the Rev. William
Crawford, 1796 or 1797. (M.R.)

Seay, Abraham, and Rosey B. Loving, spinster, November 15, 1800.
Thomas Woody, surety. Consent of her father, George Loving.

Seay, John, and Frankey Fortune, spinster, June 20, 1797. Joseph
Roberts, surety. Consent of her father, Thomas Fortune. Certificate of marriage by the Rev. William Crawford. (M.R.)

Seay, Joseph, bachelor, and Nancy Harvie, spinster, December 27,
1796. James Harvie, surety.

Sedden, William, and Rachel Stockton, married by the Rev. Benjamin
Berger, 1797?

Shackleford, Benjamin, and Frances McCullock, spinster, May 17,
1799. Benjamin Taliaferro, surety. Consent of her father, Roderick McCullock.

Shasteen, James, bachelor, and Nancey Shasteen, November 4, 1788.
William Horsley, surety. Consent of her father, John Kenedy.
Consent of Nancey.

Shasteen, Jesse, bachelor, and Ellenor Coffee, widow, November 21,
1785. Thomas Fortune, surety. Consent of Ellenor.

Shelton, Clough, bachelor, and Polly Nevil, spinster, October 15, 1798.
William B. Hare, surety. Consent of Polly. Certificate of marriage by the Rev. William Crawford. (M.R.)

Shelton, John, bachelor, and Betsey Roberts, spinster, December 10,
1789. Joseph Roberts, surety.

Shelton, Joseph, bachelor, and Mary Harris, spinster, August 1, 1785.
William Harris, surety.

Shelton, Samuel, Jr., bachelor, and Jerusha Nevil, spinster, daughter
of James Nevil, March —, 1783. James Nevil, surety.

Shenall, Thomas, and Anny Ricketts, March 1, 1792. Benjamin Plunkett, surety. Consent of her father, Thomas Ricketts.

Shenault, Caleb, and Rachel Bonds, May 28, 1795. John Bonds, surety. Consent of her father (not named). Certificate of marriage by the Rev. Lewis Dawson. (M.R.)

Shepherd, David, bachelor, and Betsey Penn, spinster, May 4, 1778. Patrick Rose, surety. Consent of her father, Gabriel Penn.

Shepherd, John, and Nancy Murrell, spinster, November 28, 1797. Charles Statham, surety. Consent of Cornelius Murrill.

Shields, David, and Elizabeth Smith, married by the Rev. William Crawford, 1797. (M.R.)

Shields, James, and Elizabeth Higginbotham [daughter of Aaron and Nancy (Croxton) Higginbotham], spinster, March 1, 1797. Elijah Brockman, surety. Consent of her mother, Nancy Higginbotham, widow. Certificate of marriage by the Rev. William Crawford. (M.R.)

Shields, William, and Nancy Lee, widow, April 14, 1782. John Penn, surety.

Shinalt, Thomas, bachelor, and Polly Jinkins, December 22, 1797. Amos Thacker, surety.

Shoemaker, Evans, bachelor, and Elizabeth Davis, spinster, December 24, 1788. George Davis, surety. Consent of his mother, Elizabeth *Shumaker,* who states that he is 21 years of age.

Shoemaker, William, and Als Mumford Peter, married by the Rev. Benjamin Coleman, March 22, 1783. (Order Book 1782-1784, p. 102.)

Shoemaker, Zedekiah, and Elizabeth Hogg, married by the Rev. Benjamin Coleman, June 12, 1783. (Order Book 1782-1784, p. 167.)

Shrader, Daniel, bachelor, and Patsey Rowsey, spinster, January 3, 1791. John Hager, surety. Consent of his father, George Shrader. Consent of Patsey, who signed as Pattey.

Shrader, George, bachelor, and Aggy Logan, spinster, June 22, 1797. Anthony Logan, surety.

Siddens, William, bachelor, and Rachel Stockton, spinster, February 8, 1797. Thomas Stockton, surety.

Simpson, James, and Mary Lancaster, April 2, 1787. David Simpson, surety. Consent of his mother, Agnes Simpson.

Sledd, Thomas, and Sally Tinsley, spinster, February 5, 1798. Thomas Grissom, surety. Consent of his father, William Sledd. Consent of her father, John Tinsley.

Sledd, William, bachelor, and Lucy Hogg, spinster, August 21, 1786. John Sledd, Jr., surety. Consent of her parents, John and Lucy Hogg.

Smith, Hillary, bachelor, of Buckingham County, and Salley Owens, spinster, April 18, 1793. Avey Owens, surety. Consent of her mother, Mary Owens. Certificate of marriage by the Rev. Mr. *Murray,* (?) April 18, 1793. (M.R.)

Smith, John, bachelor, and Elizabeth Hufman, spinster, September 9, 1779. Abraham Smith, surety. Consent of her father, Frederick Hufman.

Smith, John, bachelor, and Sally Ware, spinster, December 5, 1785. John Taliaferro, surety. Consent of her father, Edward Ware.

Smith, Phield, and Patsey Lanham, spinster, April 3, 1797. John Lanham, surety. Consent of her father, Benedick Lanham.

Smith, Wiatt, and Polly Phillips, December 24, 1799. Henry Woods, surety. Consent of her mother, Merry Phillips.

Smith, William, bachelor, and Philadelphia Franklin, spinster, November 17, 1784. Samuel Franklin, surety. Consent of Henry Franklin. Certificate of marriage by the Rev. Joseph Ballinger, November 18, 1784. (Order Book 1784-1787, p. 60.)

Smith, William, bachelor, and Haney Sneed, spinster, January 6, 1794. Randolph Sneed, surety. Consent of her father, John *Snead*.

Snead, Randolph, bachelor, and Dicey Rowsey, spinster, January 6, 1794. William Smith, surety. Consent of her father, James Rowsey.

Sneed, Benjamin, and Silvey Enicks, November 3, 1797. John Sneed, surety. David Enicks made oath that Silvey Enicks was over 21 years of age.

Sneed, John, widower, and Hannah Lane, widow, August 15, 1793. Elisha Sneed, surety. Consent of Hannah. Certificate of marriage by the Rev. William Dawson, August 15, 1793. (M.R.)

Snider, Barksdale, and Sarah Palmer, widow, February 12, 1800. John Hansard, surety. Consent of Sarah.

Snider, John, widower, and Nancy Fargason, spinster, December 11, 1784. Edward Harding, surety. Consent of Nancy. Certificate of marriage by the Rev. David Patteson, December 16, 1784. (Order Book 1784-1787, p. 68.)

Sorrel, James, and Mary McDonald, October 20, 1798. Walter Fraser, surety. Consent of James *Sorrell*, Sr. Consent of Nancy McDonald.

Speares, William, bachelor, and Anne Holladay, spinster, November 6, 1784. Thomas Penn, surety, who made oath that Anne "is at least 22 years old." Consent of Anne. Certificate of marriage by the Rev. Benjamin Coleman, December 16, 1784. (Order Book 1784-1787, p. 59.)

Spencer, James, and Mary Griffin, spinster, December 4, 1798. James Wright, surety. Consent of John M. Griffin. James Wright made oath that Mary Griffin, daughter of John Griffin, was 21 years of age. Certificate of marriage by the Rev. Walter Christian. (M.R.)

Spencer, John, and Nancy Clasby, spinster, September 25, 1799. William Clasby, surety. William Lavender made oath that John Spencer was 21 years of age. Certificate of marriage by the Rev. James Boyd. (M.R.)

pencer, Samuel, bachelor, and Nancy Stevens, spinster, January 12, 1787. James Stevens, surety.

pradling, William, and Lucy Thacher, March 7, 1796. Ambrose Thacher, surety, who made oath that Lucy Thacher, daughter of Ann Thacher, was 21 years of age.

Staples, Joseph, bachelor, and Molly Loving, spinster, March 7, 1782. John Wright, surety.

Staples, William, and Polly Hamlet, spinster (she signed as "Polly Hamblet"), November —, 1798. Parmenas Bryant, surety, who made oath that Polly was 21. Consent of Polly. Certificate of marriage by the Rev. William Crawford. (M.R.)

Statham, Thomas, bachelor, and Susannah Statham, spinster, December 21, 1795. John Phillips, surety. Consent of Ann Phillips, mother of Susanah Phillips. Certificate of marriage of Statham and *Phillips*, by the Rev. William Crawford. Bond is endorsed: "Statham & Phillips, marriage bond."

Staton, Andrew Moore, bachelor, and Amey Prewit, spinster, December 4, 1786. John Dennis Crawford, surety. Consent of his mother, Ann Staton.

Staton, Bartholomew, bachelor, and Margary Jarvis, spinster, November 12, 1787. James Frazer, surety. Consent of John Jarvis and wife, Sarah. Consent of Margary.

Staton, Bartholomew, and Sarah Jarvis, spinster, January 24, 1796. Andrew Moore Staton, surety, who made oath that Sarah was 21. Consent of her parents, John and Sarah *Jervis.*

Staton, Elijah, and Lucy Wood. Certificate of marriage by the Rev. John Shepherd, July 28, 1800. (M.R.)

Staton, James, and Mary Sorrell, July 14, 1798. James Sorrell, surety. Consent of his father, Thomas Staton, of Rockbridge County.

Staton, Reubin, bachelor, and Jane Rickets, December 1, 1795. Matthew Rickets, surety. Consent of her father, Thomas Rickets.

Staton, Thomas, bachelor, and Mary Childress, spinster, September 9, 1791. William Staton, surety. Consent of her father, John Childress.

Staton, William, and Nancy Fitzgerald, spinster, June 20, 1797. Benjamin Fitzgerald, surety, who made oath that Nancy was over 21.

Steele, William, bachelor, and Mary Dawson, spinster, December 17, 1792. Pleasant Dawson, surety. Consent of her mother, Charity Dawson. Certificate of marriage by the Rev. Mr. Dameron. (M.R.)

Stevens, James, bachelor, and Elizabeth Turner, spinster, November 25, 1785. Benjamin Powell, surety.

Stevens, John, bachelor, and Salley Turner, spinster, September 18, 1797. Teresha Turner, surety. Consent of her father, Stephen Turner. John Loving made oath that John Stevens was 21.

Stevens, Philip, and Molly Burnet, August 8, 1780. Isaac Stratton, surety. Consent of Molly.

Stennett, Joell, bachelor, and Cealia Bryant, spinster, January 4, 1790. John Bryant, surety. Consent of Benjamin Briant as to Joell Stennett.

Stennett, Reuben, bachelor, and Precilla Duggens, spinster, November 11, 1791. Alexander Duggins, Jr., surety. Consent of his father, William *Stennete*. Consent of her father, Alexander *Duggins*. Certificate of marriage by the Rev. Benjamin Coleman, November 12, 1791. (M.R.)

Stewart, Charles, bachelor, and Sally Furbush, December 15, 1785. Samuel Allen, surety. Consent of Sally.

Stewart, James, bachelor, and Clary Pollard, spinster, October 21, 1782. Charles Stewart, surety. Consent of her father, William Pollard. Certificate of marriage by the Rev. Charles Clay, October 31, 1782. (Order Book, 1782-1784, p. 107.)

Stewart, John, bachelor, and Morning Floyd, spinster, April 13, 1784. Hugh Rose, surety. Consent of her guardian, Dan Burford.

"Sir, If Capt. Stewart should be disappointed in procuring security for obtaining his license I do hereby oblige myself upon the honour of a gentm. to enter in bond with him for that purpose whenever you should require it.

Yr. friend and Obt. Servt.,

Hugh Rose.

Capt. Wm. Loving.   Geddes, Apr. 3, 1784."

Stewart, Robert, bachelor, and Sally Miles, spinster, December 5, 1792. Thomas Stewart, surety. Consent of her father, Joseph Miles. Certificate of marriage by the Rev. Mr. Crawford. (M.R.)

Stewart, Thomas, bachelor, and Tirzah Davis, widow, January 28, 1794. John Lackey, surety.

Stinchcomb, Absalom, bachelor, and Mary Penn, spinster, December 24, 1785. Joel Walker, surety. Consent of her father, Philip Penn.

Stoneham, Henry, bachelor, and Jeane Dillard, spinster, May 26, 1784. Jesse Mays, surety.

Stoneham, Henry, bachelor, and Jane Dillard, spinster, May 26, 1785. Thomas Powell, surety. Consent of her father Joseph Dillard. (See bond dated, May 26, 1784. Above.)

Stoneham, Henry, bachelor, and Rebecca Powell, spinster, February 12, 1785. Thomas Powell (Taylor) surety. Consent of his father, George Stoneham. Consent of her father, John Powell.

Stovall, George (minor), and Anna Mitchell, spinster, January 6, 1778. Joseph Cooper, surety. Consent of her father, Archelaus Mitchell.

Stratton, Henry, and Barbary Wilsher, married by the Rev. Benjamin Coleman, December 16, 1784. (Order Book 1784-1787, p. 59.)

Stratton, Jacob, bachelor, and Elizabeth Whittle, spinster, April 24, 1789. Charles Welsher (Wilsher?), surety.

Stratton, James, and Elizabeth Blair, spinster, February 19 1799. Spotswood Garland, surety. Certificate of marriage by the Rev. Walter Christian. (M.R.)

Stratton, William, bachelor, and Milly Wright, spinster, July 24, 1796. William Lavender, surety. Consent of her father, Jesse Wright.

Suddeath, Jarrott, bachelor, and Meney Puckett, spinster, August 27, 1790. Jacob Pucket, surety. Consent of her father, Jacob *Pucket,* who calls her *Myney* Pucket.

Sullivan, George, of Lynchburg, and Sarah Cox, spinster, November 25, 1800. Robert Tinsley, surety. Consent of her father, Valentine Cox.

Swann, Leven, bachelor, and Elizabeth Jenkins, spinster, January 6, 1791. Thomas Jenkins, surety.

Swason, John, and Mary Knight, spinster, January 28, 1800. Joseph Ship, surety. Consent of her parents, John and Caty Knight.

Sweet, John Lenard, and Jenny O. Bryant, widow, March 22, 1797. James Hamilton, surety. Consent of Jenny O. Certificate of marriage by the Rev. Ro: Jones. (M.R.)

Swingleton, William, widower, and Elizabeth Mullins, widow, July 24, 1784. William Wright, Jr., surety. Consent of her father, Christian Hooten, who calls her "Elizabeth Mullings." Consent of Elizabeth, who signs as Elizabeth *Mullin.*

Swinney, Henry, bachelor, and Anne Martin, spinster, April 2, 1787. John Martin, surety. Consent of his mother, Elizabeth Swinney.

Swinney, Joseph, and Nanney Whitten, married by the Rev. Benjamin Coleman, December 5, 1782. (Order Book 1782-1784, p. 73.)

Taliaferro, Benjamin, and Martha Meriwether, April 8, 1782. Edmund Wilcox, surety. Consent of her father, David *Merriwether.*

Taliaferro, Benjamin, bachelor, and Mildred Taylor, spinster, January 23, 1792. John Taliaferro, surety. Consent of her father, James Franklin.

Taliaferro, Charles, Jr., bachelor, and Lucy Loving, spinster, May 20, 1785. John Loving, surety.

Taliaferro, John, bachelor, and Betsy Loving, spinster, January 13, 1787. William Loving, Jr., surety.

Taliaferro, Richard, bachelor, and Mildred Powell, spinster, July 18, 1780. William Powell, surety. Consent of her father, Lucas Powell.

Taliaferro, William, and Nancy N. Eubank, spinster, November 17, 1800. Thomas N. Eubank, surety. Consent of her father, John Eubank.

Taliaferro, Zacharias, widower, and Judith Horsley, widow, March 17, 1787. Lucas Powell, surety. Consent of Judith.

Taliaferro, Zacharias, bachelor, and Sally Warwick, seamstress, June 16, 1790. Benjamin Taliaferro, surety. Consent of her father, Abraham Warwick.

Tankersley, Joseph, and Milley Brown, widow, December 25, 1800. Solomon Carter, surety.

Tarrant, Leonard, and Mary Hargrove, May 6, 1771. William Loving, surety. Consent of Mary.

Tate, William, bachelor, and Lucy Phillips, spinster, January 7, 1793. James Phillips, surety. Consent of her father, John Phillips.

Taylor, George, bachelor, and Ann Waters, spinster, married by the Rev. Charles Clay, May 22, 1783. (Order Book 1782-1784, p. 136.)

Taylor, George, bachelor, and Agnes Lunceford, spinster, February 23, 1790. Joshua Doss, surety. Consent of his father, Will Taylor. Consent of her father, William Lunceford.

Taylor, Henry, bachelor, and Mary Taylor, spinster, December 24, 1794. George Lunsford, surety. Consent of her father, John Taylor. Certificate of marriage by the Rev. Ezekiel Campbell. (M.R.)

Taylor, James, bachelor, and Sarah Hix, spinster, December 31, 1793. John Childress, Jr., surety.

Taylor, Jeremiah, widower, and Anne Stovall, widow, December 4, 1783. Thomas Powell (Taylor), surety. Consent of her mother, Ann Stovall.

Teas, William, and Mary Reid, spinster, May 7, 1770. Alexander Reid, Jr., surety. Consent of Mary.

Teas, William, and Sarah Loving, spinster, July 21, 1798. William Vaughan, surety. Consent of her father, John Loving. Certificate of marriage by the Rev. William Crawford. (M.R.)

Telford, Joseph, bachelor, and Nancy Jones, spinster, June 5, 1787. George Wooddy, surety. Consent of her mother, Mary Ann Jones.

Tennison, Henry, bachelor, and Peggy Alley, spinster, October 24, 1795. Thomas Ridgway, surety. Consent of her father, Josiah Alley.

Tennison, Levy, bachelor, and Phebe Robinson, spinster, December 14, 1787. John Tennison, surety. Consent of her father, John Robinson.

Terrant, John, and Tabitha Tankersly, December 7, 1768. Benjamin Pollard, surety. Consent of Richard Tankersley.

Thacker, Joel, and Sally Burford, May 3, 1797. William Burford, surety.

Thomas, Daniel, bachelor, and Behethland Wortham, spinster, December 19, 1792. Thomas Appling, surety. Consent of Thomas Wortham. James Thomas made oath that Daniel Thomas was over 21.

Thomas, David, bachelor, and Nancy Gatewood, spinster, April 7, 1789. Ambrose Gatewood, surety.

Thomas, James, bachelor, and Elisabeth Roberts, spinster, May 3, 1786. John Thomas, surety. Consent of Ellot Roberts and Elizabeth Roberts.

Thomas, James, widower, and Patty Gregory, spinster, August 30, 1794. Henry Read, surety, who made oath that Patty was over 21.

Thomas, John, bachelor, and Jane Skinnell, widow, August 21, 1790. Jabus Davis, surety. Consent of Jane.

Thomas, Norborn, bachelor, and Judith Wiatt, seamstress, May 21, 1791. James Nevil, surety. Consent of her father, John Wiatt, who stated she was under age.

Thompson, Archibald, bachelor, and Milley Griffin, spinster, April 26, 1785. George Purvis, Jr., surety. Consent of his father, Robert Thompson. Consent of her father, Thomas Griffin.

Thompson, David, bachelor, of Augusta County, and Charlott Hansbrough, spinster, March 19, 1788. Consent of her mother, Keziah Hansbrough.

Thompson, George, and Sally Philips, married by the Rev. William Crawford, 1796 or 1797. (M.R.)

Thompson, James, bachelor, and Elizabeth Stephens, spinster, October 14, 1795. Thomas Spencer, surety. Consent of her father, James *Stevens*. Certificate of marriage by the Rev. William Crawford. (M.R.)

Thompson, James, bachelor, and Winney Davis, spinster, February 26, 1790. John Thompson, surety. Consent of her mother, Hannah Davis, widow.

Thompson, James, and Mary Thompson. See bond of John Thompson and Mary Thompson.

Thompson, Jesse, and Judith Martin, November 5, 1792. Andrew Wright, surety. Consent of her father, Peter Martin.

Thompson, John (minor), and Mary Thompson, spinster, February 4, 1800. John Thompson, surety. James Thompson, Sr., requests the Clerk to issue a marriage license to *James Thompson* (minor), and Mary Thompson. John Thompson made oath that *James* Thompson was over 21. Certificate of marriage of *James* Thompson and Mary Thompson, by the Rev. James Floyd. (M.R.)

Thompson, John, bachelor, and Judith Wills, spinster, September 10, 1791. Samuel Hill. surety. Consent of her father, James Wills, Sr.

Thompson, John, bachelor, and Rebecah Edwards Powell, spinster, December 9, 1786. Nathaniel Powell, surety. Consent of her father, Lucas Powell.

Thompson, John, Jr., and Caroline E. Brown, February 20, 1800. This is an authorization only, issued by the Clerk of the Court and not a bond.

Thompson, Joseph, bachelor, and Sally Phillips, December 28, 1796. John Phillips, surety.

Thompson, Mitchell, bachelor, and Mary Griffin, spinster, October 13, 1784. No surety named. Consent of his father, Robert Thompson. Consent of her father, Thomas Griffin. Certificate of marriage by the Rev. David Patteson, October 14, 1784. (Order Book 1784-1787, p. 1.)

Thornton, Peter Presley, bachelor, and Mary McCullock, spinster, May 10, 1792. Consent of her father, Roderick McCullock. Certificate of marriage by the Rev. Mr. Crawford. (M.R.)

Thurmond, Felix, and Elizabeth Hill, married by the Rev. Benjamin Coleman, October 10, 1783. (Order Book 1782-1784, p. 201.)

Tiller, John, bachelor, and Nancey Tiller, daughter of William Tiller, June 10, 1784. John Wright, surety. Consent of her father, Thomas Hopper (step-father?). Consent of Nansey Hopper.

Tiller, William, widower, and Sarah Saunders, widow, July 17, 1790. William Teas, surety. Consent of Sarah, who signs as Sarah *Sanders.*

Tindall, John, bachelor, of Buckingham County, and Nancy Turner, spinster, November 18, 1798. James Stephens, surety. Consent of her father Stephen Turner.

Tindol, Lewis, and Lucy Allen, spinster, February 18, 1793. George Allen, surety. Consent of Samuel Allen.

Tinsley, Anthony, and Judith Cox, spinster, March 5, 1798. Martin Dawson, Jr., surety. Consent of his father, John Tinsley, who states that he is of age. Consent of her father, Volentine Cox.

Tinsley, Edward, bachelor, and Lucy Tinsley, spinster, January 8, 1789. Jacob Tyree, Jr., surety. Consent of his father, John Tinsley. Consent of her father, David Tinsley.

Tinsley, George, and Susanna Dawson, spinster, March 11, 1799. Nelson C. Dawson, surety. Consent of her father, Martin Dawson.

Tinsley, James, and Sally Hardwick, September 28, 1796. Ambrose Rucker, Jr., surety. Richard Hardwick made oath that Sally was 21. Consent of Sally, stating she was of age.

Tinsley, Moses, and Betsey Turner, March 19, 1798. John Turner, surety.

Tinsley, Reubin, bachelor, and Fanny Tyree, spinster, May 2, 1786. Richard Lee, surety.

Tinsley, Richard, bachelor, and Sarah Burks, spinster, September 10, 1794. James Tinsley, surety. Consent of her guardian, Charles Burks.

Tomlinson, William, and Betsey Clements, spinster, February 17, 1800. John Clements, surety, who made oath that William *Tomblinson* was over 21. Consent of William Clements.

Toney, Reuben, bachelor, and Fanny Willoughby, widow, December 12, 1792. Samuel Megehee, surety. Consent of Fanny.

Tongate, Martin, and Susannah Fraser, spinster, October 4, 1800. Walter Fraser, surety. Consent of her mother, Marget Fraser.

Certificate of marriage by the Rev. John Young, October 9, 1800. (M.R.)

Tooley, John, and Milley Witt, December 10, 1796. David Witt, surety. Consent of her mother, Jean Witt.

Trayley, Francis, bachelor, and Sarah Jones, spinster, June 10, 1786. Thomas Beddow, surety. Consent of Sarah.

Trent, John B., bachelor, and Patsy Mitchell, spinster, January 2, 1792. Samuel Hill, surety. Consent of her father, Archelaus Mitchell.

Triall, David, bachelor, and Mary Turner, spinster, January 4, 1791. James Murphy, surety. Consent of her father, Stephen Turner.

Tucker, Daniel, bachelor, and Judith Coleman, widow, September 15, 1792. Robert Tucker, surety. Consent of Judith. Certificate of marriage by the Rev. Mr. Crawford. (M.R.)

Tucker, Drury, and Frances Lee, widow, April 6, 1767. George Penn, surety. Consent of Frances.

Tucker, Isaac, and Elizabeth Major, spinster, December 23, 1799. Zachariah Tucker, surety. Consent of her mother, Lucy Major.

Tucker, Jesse, bachelor, and Nancy Layne, spinster, January 10, 1791. Garland Hurt, surety. Consent of her father, Henry Layne, Jr.

Tucker, John, bachelor, and Rhoda Powell, spinster, December 5, 1778. John Ennis, surety. Consent of her guardian, Wiatt Powell. Consent of Rhoda.

Tucker, Joseph, and Catherine Barnes, spinster, ————, 1772 (day and month not given). Edmund Wilcox, surety.

Tucker, Matthew, widower, and Esther Stamps, widow, December 15, 1787. Cornelius Sale, surety. Consent of Matthew and Esther.

Tucker, Robert, bachelor, and Phebe Ballinger, spinster, August 6, 1791. Daniel Tucker, surety. Consent of her father, Joseph Ballinger.

Tuley, Charles, and Polly Witt, spinster, September 6, 1800. John Tuley, surety. Consent of his mother, Elizabeth *Twoley*. Consent of her mother, Jinney Witt.

Tuly, John, and Milly Witt, married by the Rev. William Crawford, 1796 or 1797. (M.R.)

Tungate, James, bachelor, and Ann Hall, spinster, December 24, 1792. Robert Buttry, surety. Consent of her father, Moses Hall. James Tungate made oath that Ann Hall was about 21.

Tunget, Fielding, and Easter Wilson, married by the Rev. Benjamin Coleman, January 29, 1783. (Order Book 1782-1784, p. 102.)

Tungett, John, bachelor, and Betsey Rice, spinster, December 5, 1791. John Clements, surety. Consent of his father, Jeremiah *Tungate*. Consent of her father, Edward Rice. Certificate of marriage by the Rev. Benjamin Coleman, December 6, 1792. He calls him John *Tungate*. (M.R.)

Turner, James, Jr., and Lucy Ham, spinster, November 28, 1795. Stephen Ham [her father], surety. Certificate of marriage by the Rev. Charles Crawford. (M.R.)

Turner, John, bachelor, and Elizabeth Bailey, spinster, June 14, 1791. John Bailey, surety.

Turner, Samuel, bachelor, and Sarah Spencer, spinster, August 3, 1789. William Spencer, surety.

Turner, Terisha, bachelor, and Elizabeth Thomas, spinster, August 16, 1780. James Nevil, surety. Consent of his father, Stephen Turner. Consent of her father, James Thomas, of Cumberland County.

Turner, Thomas, bachelor, and Anna Rodes Martin, spinster, October 5, 1793. Thomas Martin, surety. Consent of her parents, Azh. (Azariah) and Mary Martin, who state she is in her 20th year.

Turpin, Philip, of Powhatan County, bachelor, and Caroline Rose, seamstress, October 5, 1787. Charles Rose, surety. Consent of Hugh Rose, who calls Philip Turpin "Physician of the County of Powhatan."

Tyler, John, bachelor, and Elizabeth Dillard, spinster, February 2, 1789. William Oglesby, surety. Consent of his father, Charles Tyler. Consent of her father, William Dillard. Consent of Elizabeth.

Tyree, William, bachelor, and Frances McDaniel, spinster, December 5, 1785. George McDaniel, surety.

Upshaw, John and Amey Gatewood, spinster, March 5, 1776. James Pamplin, surety.

Vaughan, Cornelius, bachelor, and Nancy Carter, spinster, November 11, 1778. William Carter, surety. Consent of his guardian, Joseph Edmunds, who states that Nancy Carter is a daughter of Job Carter.

Vaughan, George, bachelor, and Sucky Loving, spinster, December 24, 1795. George Woody, surety. Consent of Betty Loving. Certificate of marriage by the Rev. William Crawford. (M.R.)

Vaughan, William, bachelor, of Culpeper County, and Elizabeth Loving, spinster, January 5, 1789. Consent of her father, John Loving.

Veal, Nathan, widower, and Jane Milstead, spinster, August 18, 1785. William Carter, surety. Consent of her parents, Joseph and Rebecca Milstead.

Wade, Daniel, and Linney Witt, spinster, October 4, 1798. William Thorpe, surety. Consent of his mother, Nancy Morris. Consent of George Morris, as to Daniel Wade. Consent of her father, David Witt. Certificate of marriage by the Rev. William Crawford. (M.R.)

Wade, Edwin H., and Charlotte Thompson, widow, December 19, 1800. Peter Campbell, surety. (Bond reads Edwin H. *Waide.*)

Walker, Joel, and Mary Penn, spinster, February 21, 1775. Samuel Allen, surety. Consent of Mary.

Walker, Robert, bachelor, and Nancy Powell, spinster, April 30, 1792. Owen Haskins, surety. Consent of her father, Wiatt Powell. Certificate of marriage by the Rev. Mr. Crawford. (M.R.)

Walrond, Benjamin, and Patsey Wiley, March 28, 1796. William Robinson, surety, who made oath that Patsey was 21. Certificate of marriage by the Rev. Lewis Dawson. (M.R.)

Walters, John, bachelor, and Mary Smith, spinster, December 29, 1794. Charles Smith, surety. Consent of her parents, William and Elizabeth Smith. Certificate of marriage by the Rev. Benjamin Berger.

Walton, William, and Mildred Lavender, April 16, 1792. William Lavender, surety. Consent of Mildred.

Ware, Edward, Jr., and Sally Thurmond, May 6, 1782. John Ware, surety. Consent of her father, Philip Thurmond. Certificate of marriage by the Rev. Benjamin Coleman, May 7, 1782. (Order Book 1773-1782, p. 512.)

Ware, James, and Nancy Pendleton, spinster, December 13, 1800. James Garland, surety. Consent of his father, John Ware. Consent of her father, Reubin Pendleton.

Ware, James, bachelor, and Mary Veale, spinster, October 19, 1782. Thomas Waugh, surety. Consent of her father, Carneby *Veal.* Consent of Mary. Certificate of marriage by the Rev. Charles Clay, October 24, 1782. (Order Book 1782-1784, p. 107.)

Ware, John, bachelor, and Lucy Eubanks, spinster, September 12, 1796. John Eubanks, surety.

Ware, Seth, and Rebecca Griffin, spinster, July 24, 1799. Harrison Griffin, surety. Consent of her parents, John and Rebecca Griffin, who state she is of full age.

Ware, William, and Patty Davis, spinster, December 29, 1777. Thomas Waugh, surety. Consent of Patty.

Warner, Samuel, widower, and Elizabeth Miller, spinster, February 23, 1786. James Brooks, surety. Consent of her mother, Sarah Miller.

Warren, Abraham, bachelor, and Rebecca Staton, spinster, January 20, 1794. Jacob Petty John, surety, who made oath that Rebecca Staton, daughter of William Staton, deceased, was over 20. Certificate of marriage by the Rev. William Dameron, February 4, 1794. (M.R.)

Warren, James, bachelor, and Levicey Bryant, spinster, November 14, 1795. William Bryant, surety.

Warren, John, bachelor, and Betsey Blankenship, spinster, February 13, 1794. William Clark, surety. Consent of her father, Noel Blankenship. Certificate of marriage by the Rev. William Dameron, February 14, 1794. (M.R.)

Warwick, Beverley, bachelor, and Elizabeth Martin, spinster, daughter of Henry Martin, February 26, 1781. John Martin, surety.

Watkins, John, bachelor, and Anne Redman, spinster, August 26, 1795. George Redman, surety. Certificate of marriage by the Rev. Charles Crawford. (M.R.)

Watts, Benjamin, and Fanny Lee, spinster, March 24, 1800. William Lee, surety. Consent of her brother and guardian, James Lee.

Watts, Charles, bachelor, and Elizabeth Dillard, spinster, January 4, 1790. James Dillard, surety.

Watts, John, and Elizabeth Wilcox, spinster, April 22, 1799. Thomas Wilcox, surety. Consent of his father, Caleb Watts, who stated his son was 21 and that he was willing he should marry "Elizabeth Wilcox, daughter of Thomas Wilcox."

Watts, Stephen, Planter, and Elizabeth Farrar, spinster, June 30, 1772. William Spencer, surety, who testifies that Elizabeth is of lawful age. Consent of Elizabeth.

Watts, Stephen, widower, and Martha Christian, widow, January 24, 1790. Charles Watts, surety. Consent of Martha to marry "Captain Stephen Watts."

Watts, William Lawson, and Mary Ann Dillard, spinster, March 17, 1800. John Camm, surety.

Waugh, George, bachelor, and Susannah Brown, spinster, December 20, 1794. Henry Waugh, surety. Consent of her mother, Susanna Brown, the elder, who states she is of lawful age.

Waugh, Henry, bachelor, and Elizabeth Brown, spinster, June 21, 1794. George Waugh, surety. Consent of Susanna Brown. Certificate of marriage by the Rev. William Dameron, July 26, 1794. (M.R.)

Waugh, James, bachelor, and Sally Tinsley, widow, December 3, 1792. William Parks, surety. Consent of his father, Thomas Waugh. Consent of Sally. Certificate of marriage by the Rev. Mr. Crawford. (M.R.)

Waugh, Richard, and Pamelia Campbell, spinster, September 1, 1798. John Camm, surety. Consent of her father, Laurence Campbell.

Webb, William, and Polly Taylor, spinster, September 14, 1799. Thomas Taylor, surety. Consent of her father, Edward Taylor. Thomas Taylor made oath that William Webb was upwards of 21. Certificate of marriage by the Rev. John Young, September 17, 1799. (M.R.)

Weir, Andrew, bachelor, and Jane Reid, spinster, September 1, 1788. John N. Reid, surety. Consent of her father, Alexander Reid.

Weise, George, bachelor, and Fanny King, spinster, December 6, 1786. John Taliaferro, surety. Consent of her father, Joseph King.

Weise, John George, and Elizabeth Harrison, spinster, August 14, 1797. John Vasen (he signs as "Johan Waaser"), surety.

Welch, Joseph, bachelor, and Susannah Harper, widow, December 15, 1785. John Profitt, surety. Consent of Susannah.

Welch, Robert, bachelor, and Mary Horsley, spinster, September 3, 1794. John Ray, surety, who testified that Mary Horsley was over 21.

Welsh, Andrew, and Henrietta Maria Parrott, married by the Rev. Benjamin Coleman, September 2, 1783. (Order Book 1782-1784, p. 201.)

West, Bransford, bachelor, and Nancy Joplin, spinster, March 3, 1792. Consent of her mother, Cate *Jopling*. John West, surety.

West, Francis, bachelor, and Ruth Becknall, spinster, January 7, 1790. John Wood, surety. Consent of Ruth.

West, Nicholas, bachelor, and Betsey Tinsley, spinster, November 18, 1793. Battaile Harrison, surety. Consent of her father, John Tinsley. Certificate of marriage by the Rev. Mr. Crawford. (M.R.)

Westbrook, William, bachelor, and Nancy Henderson, spinster, June 16, 1790. John Fortune, surety. Consent of Nancy.

Wharton, George, bachelor, of Albemarle County, and Elizabeth Harris, spinster, November 10, 1792. William Harris, surety. Consent of her father, Matthew Harris, Sr.

White, Arthur, of Albemarle County, and Suckey Magann, spinster, October 16, 1777. Joseph Megann and Edmund Wilcox, sureties. Consent of her father (not named). Consent of Suckey.

White, Benjamin, bachelor, and Nancy Goodwin, spinster, July 10, 1787. Consent of her father, Micajah Goodwin.

White, Conyers, bachelor, of Albemarle County, and Frances Roberts, spinster, December 1, 1788. Zachariah Roberts, surety. Consent of her parents, Henry and Elizabeth Roberts.

White, Cornelius, bachelor, and Catherine Hall, spinster, November 2, 1789. William Hall, surety. Consent of her father, Moses Hall.

White, Joseph, of Orange County, bachelor, and Prisellah Dawson, spinster, January 8, 1793. Martin Dawson, surety. Consent of her father, John Dawson.

White, Joseph, and Coatney Cooper, spinster, March 13, 1799. John Camm, surety. Her brother, Robert *Cowper*, made oath that Coatney was 21.

White, Samuel, bachelor, of Campbell County, and Fanny Penn, spinster, November 6, 1793. James M. Brown, surety. Consent of her father, Gabriel Penn.

White, Zachariah, and Sarah Mays, spinster, February 10, 1800. James Mays, surety. Certificate of marriage by the Rev. William Crawford. (M.R.)

Whitehead, Burcher, bachelor, and Nancey Camden, spinster, December 1, 1788. Henry Camden, surety.

Whitehead, Richard, and Spencey Campden, October 26, 1795. Thomas Powell, surety. Consent of her father, William Campden. Certificate of marriage by the Rev. Charles Crawford. (M.R.)

Whitesides, James, bachelor, and Ann Kinney, spinster, August 7, 1792. James McCune, surety. Consent of his father, John Whitesides, of Albemarle County, who states that his son is under 21. Consent of her father, William Kinney, Jr. Certificate of marriage by the Rev. Mr. Campbell. (M.R.)

Whitten, Berry, bachelor, and Frankey Gatewood, spinster, November 17, 1786. James Nowlan, surety. Consent of her father, Ambrose Gatewood.

Wickersham, James, bachelor, and Sally Plunkett, spinster, January 7, 1793. Ambrose Rucker, Jr., surety. Consent of Benjamin Plunkett [her father]. Certificate of marriage by the Rev. William Crawford. (M.R.)

Wilborn, William, bachelor, and Eda Guttry, spinster, April 2, 1787. Benjamin Miln, surety. Consent of his father, William Wilborn. Consent of her father, William Guttry.

Wilkerson, Stith, bachelor, and Polley Bowman, spinster, January 19, 1791. John Ball, surety. Consent of her father, William Bowman.

Wilkinson, John, bachelor, and Lusithay Bowman, spinster, April 22, 1794. John ˌBowman, surety. Consent of her father, William Bowman.

Williams, Roger, and Cassean Blair, spinster, February 22, 1775. Allen Blair, surety. Consent of her father, William Blair.

Willoughby, Joshua, bachelor, and Elizabeth Saunders, spinster, April 15, 1789. William Allen, surety. Consent of her mother, Sary Saunders.

Wills, James, and Betsy Warwick, October 3, 1795. Consent of her father, Abraham Warwick. This is a consent only. Certificate of marriage by the Rev. William Crawford. (M.R.)

Wilmore, James, widower, and Nancy Mahon, spinster, November 27, 1790. John Mahon, surety. Consent of her father, William Mahon.

Wilmore, James, and Betsy Dillard, married by the Rev. W. Crawford, *1800?* (M.R.)

Willmore, William, and Nancy Harrison, spinster, August 28, 1798. Reubin Harrison, surety. James Wilmore made oath that William Willmore was 23 years old. Consent of her mother, Sally Harrison.

Wilsher, John, bachelor, and Sally Wilsher, spinster, October 3, 1796. James Warren, surety. Consent of her father, Richard Wilsher, who stated she was 21.

Wilsher, Joseph, and Sally Rutherford, widow, April 28, 1798. Jacob Tyree, surety. Certificate of marriage by the Rev. Walter Christian. (M.R.)

Wilson, Benjamin, and Elizabeth Clark, December 22, 1795. Robert Robinson, surety. Consent of her father, Micajah *Clarke.* Certificate of marriage by the Rev. Lewis Dawson. (M.R.)

Wilson, James, and Betsey Dillard. On a "List of Marriages performed by the Rev. William Crawford, between Oct., 1799, and Jan., 1800."

Wilson, James, bachelor, and Margaret Bowler, spinster, December 6, 1786. William Wilson, surety. Consent of his parents, William and Sarah Wilson, who state that he is 23. Consent of her parents, James and Mary Bowler.

Wilson, William, and Nancy Hartless, October 8, 1798. Thomas Allen, surety, who made oath that Nancy was 21. Consent of Nancy.

Wiltshire, Thomas, bachelor, and Sarah Goff, spinster, July 28, 1792. Jonathan Dakin, surety. Consent of John Burford, Sr., for Thomas *Wilcher* to marry Sarah Goff.

Wingfield, Ro., and Nancy Wingfield, spinster, February 18, 1799. Nathan Wingfield, surety. Certificate of marriage by the Rev. Walter Christian. (M.R.)

Witt, Dennett Abny, bachelor, and Conney Oglesby, spinster, January 4, 1790. David Witt, surety. Consent of Richard Oglesby.

Witt, Littleberry, and Jenny Burnett, September 30, 1777. Daniel Witt, surety.

Wood, Alexander, and Caty Steel, married by the Rev. Benjamin Coleman, October 28, 1784. (Order Book 1784-1787, p. 59.)

Wood, Henry, bachelor, and Ann Bowls, widow, September 4, 1786. Joseph Goodwin, surety. "I Anny Boyles of Amherst County being a widow of thirty years old have given Leave for Henry Wood of the said County to take out Lisons.
Sept. 4, 1786. Anny Boyles."

Wood, Jacob, and Bartheene Phillips, February 16, 1796. William Tyree, surety. Consent of her father, William Phillips. Certificate of marriage by the Rev. William Crawford. (M.R.)

Wood, Jesse, and Nancy Hamlet, spinster, November 7, 1797. Robert Grant, surety. Consent of her mother, Susana *Hamblet.* Certificate of marriage by the Rev. William Crawford. (M.R.)

Wood, John, bachelor, and Mary Wright, spinster, January 11, 1784. John Wright, surety. Consent of her father, Robert Wright.

Wood, Richard, bachelor, and Hannah Jopling, spinster, January 5, 1785. William Wright, Jr., surety. Consent of her father, Josiah Jopling. Consent of his father, Josias Wood.

Woodroof, David, Jr., and Judy McDaniel, January 19, 1800. Richard Jones, surety. Consent of her father, John McDaniel, dated October 3, 1799.

Woodroof, Jesse, bachelor, and Judith Lee, spinster, August 1, 1791. John Woodroof, surety. Consent of his father, David Woodroof. Consent of John Wiatt. (Joseph and Susanna Dawson also signed.) Consent of Judith.

Woodroof, Wiatt, bachelor, and Dorothy Digges, spinster, July 9, 1794. David S. Garland, surety. Judith Tucker made oath that Dorothy Digges, daughter of John Digges, of Amherst County, was 21.

Woods, Samuel, widower, and Sarah Rice, spinster, December 25, 1779. John Loving, Jr., surety.

Woods, William, of Albemarle County, and Ann Reid, widow, September 19, 1800. Samuel Reid, surety. Certificate of marriage by the Rev. Benjamin Berger, September 25, 1800. (M.R.)

Woody, Thomas, and Nancy Griffin, December 15, 1800. Abraham Seay, surety. Consent of her mother, Susanna Griffin.

Wortham, Notley, and Susanna Maddox, February 2, 1799. George Wortham, surety.

Wray, John, bachelor, and Ruthe Robertson, spinster, December 16, 1791. Augustin Proffit, surety. Consent of her father, Arthur Robertson.

Wren, John, bachelor, and Elizabeth Johnson, spinster, November 22, 1791. John Moran, surety. Consent of her father, Stephen Johnson.

Wright, Andrew, widower, and Lucy Childress, daughter of Benjamin Childress, March 10, 1779. William Wright, Jr., surety. Consent of her mother, Ann Childress, who states Lucy is of lawful age. Consent of Lucy.

Wright, David, and Polly Burks, spinster, October 18, 1798. William Stratton, surety, who made oath that Polly was 21. Certificate of marriage by the Rev. Walter Christian. (M.R.)

Wright, George, bachelor, and Elizabeth Landrum, spinster, January 19, 1789. Young Landrum, surety.

Wright, James, widower, and Ann Medeares, widow, January 4, 1792. Hudson Martin, surety. Consent of Ann.

Wright, James, and Lucy Crisp, spinster, February 1, 1800. John Crisp, surety. Consent of her parents, William and Lucy Crisp.

Wright, Jesse, bachelor, and Dicy Gillaspie, spinster, October 28, 1794. Lewis Gillaspie, surety. Consent of her father, George Gillaspie.

Wright, Jesse, and Susannah Harper, spinster, January 6, 1772. William Welch, surety. Consent of Susannah.

Wright, Jesse, widower, and Rachel Welch, spinster, April 6, 1784. Roderick McCullock, surety. Consent of her father, John Welch.

Wright, John, and Mary Smith, August 1, 1781. Consent of Mary stating she is of lawful age. Thomas Johnson made oath that Mary was above 21. This is a consent only. There is no M.L.B. of record.

Wright, John, and Mary Mellon, spinster, May 22, 1798. Bartlett Eads, surety, who made oath that John Wright, son of Robert Wright, was 21.

Wright, John, bachelor, and Nancy Melton, spinster, May 21, 1797. Consent of her father, John Melton. This is a consent only. There is no M.L.B. of record.

Wright, John, bachelor, and Susannah Bibb, spinster, October 9, 1789. William Bibb, surety.

Wright, Lindsey, and Elizabeth Wilcher, spinster, August 27, 1799. John Wilcher, surety. Consent of his father, Jessey (Jesse) Wright. Certificate of marriage by the Rev. Walter Christian, August 29, 1799. (M.R.)

Wright, Maurice, and Molly Lawless, September 29, 1797. William Lawless, surety. Consent of her father, Richard Lawless. Certificate of marriage by the Rev. Charles Crawford.

Wright, Robert, bachelor, and Keziah Bibb, spinster, November 2, 1784. William Bibb, surety. Certificate of marriage by the Rev. Joseph Ballinger, November 25, 1784. (Order Book 1784-1787, p. 60.)

Wright, Samuel, bachelor, and Nancy Gatewood, spinster, November 8, 1791. Charles Christian, surety. Consent of her mother, Sarah Gatewood.

Wright, William, bachelor, and Frances Hudson, spinster, December 12, 1793. Reubin Hudson, surety. Consent of her father, Rush Hudson.

Wright, William, Jr., bachelor, and Margaret Johnson, spinster, November 21, 1787. John Wright, surety. Consent of her father, John Johnson.

Yancey, Robert, and Ann Crawford, spinster, November 14, 1767. Charles Yancey, surety. Consent of Ann.

Yellow, William, and Salley Mays, married by the Rev. Benjamin Coleman, September 30, 1784. (Order Book 1784-1787, p. 1.)

INDEX

This index contains the names of the women only, as the bonds are arranged alphabetically in the names of the men.

98 INDEX

www.ingramcontent.com/pod-product-compliance
Lightning Source LLC
Chambersburg PA
CBHW070513090426
42735CB00012B/2759